S. Hrg. 114–327

INDEPENDENT SOUTH SUDAN: A FAILURE OF LEADERSHIP

HEARING

BEFORE THE

COMMITTEE ON FOREIGN RELATIONS UNITED STATES SENATE

ONE HUNDRED FOURTEENTH CONGRESS

FIRST SESSION

DECEMBER 10, 2015

Printed for the use of the Committee on Foreign Relations

Available via the World Wide Web: http://www.gpo.gov/fdsys/

U.S. GOVERNMENT PUBLISHING OFFICE

21–183 PDF   WASHINGTON : 2016

For sale by the Superintendent of Documents, U.S. Government Publishing Office
Internet: bookstore.gpo.gov   Phone: toll free (866) 512–1800; DC area (202) 512–1800
Fax: (202) 512–2104   Mail: Stop IDCC, Washington, DC 20402–0001

(II)

CONTENTS

INDEPENDENT SOUTH SUDAN: A FAILURE OF LEADERSHIP

Thursday, December 10, 2015

U.S. SENATE,
COMMITTEE ON FOREIGN RELATIONS,
Washington, DC.

The committee met, pursuant to notice, at 10:00 a.m., in Room SD–419, Dirksen Senate Office Building, Hon. Bob Corker, chairman of the committee, presiding.

Present: Senators Corker [presiding], Cardin, and Kaine.

OPENING STATEMENT OF HON. BOB CORKER, U.S. SENATOR FROM TENNESSEE

The CHAIRMAN. The Foreign Relations Committee meeting will come to order. We want to thank everyone for being here.

A decade after the United States helped regional leaders coax the warring sides of Sudan and now South Sudan to end the decades-long war that displaced and killed millions, the very same type of violence has returned to the region under this new and independent leadership.

Today's hearing will examine the prospect for stabilizing the deadly, manmade crisis that has again destroyed the lives and hopes of millions of innocent people in South Sudan.

The peace agreement signed in August offers a vehicle by which the parties responsible for this catastrophe might change the trajectory of their country. Our witnesses will provide the status of U.S. efforts to reverse this post-independence descent into violence. I hope they will also explain how we ended up in such a complex crisis after the U.S. and international community invested so much in a seeming resolution to civil war.

Why has the leadership of the current president and the former vice president chosen to mimic the maligned policies of ethnic hatred and targeting of civilians to tear apart their newly independent country? With 1.6 million people displaced internally and an additional 750,000 having fled the country, how do these purported leaders justify their involvement in fomenting such bloodshed and the resulting humanitarian crisis?

There are an unprecedented 4 level-3 humanitarian emergencies occurring right now in Syria, Iraq, Yemen, and South Sudan that are testing the world's capacity to muster an effective response, despite the direct interference on the ground.

This hearing is an opportunity to further expose the atrocities emerging from the region and appeal to better governance, for the sake of 12 million citizens of South Sudan and its neighbors.

In addition to a significant grassroots advocacy by constituents here at home and diplomatic engagement involving numerous Secretaries of State and the President, we have also dedicated billions of dollars to help establish an independent South Sudan that is free to achieve its potential in a nation blessed with resources. Nonetheless, after such considerable investment, the United States continues to commit to peace, contributing over $1.3 billion in humanitarian aid in the last 2 years alone.

I hope we are learning from our experience over the years here and elsewhere to engage more effectively and otherwise identify and address the key obstacles to sustainable peace that have eluded us this time. I look forward to hearing what might be done to end the disturbing violence and restore stable, responsible governance in this sad and repetitive case, and what mechanisms might be employed to improve the international influence toward better outcomes in the future.

Also I wish to note the presence of officials from the Embassy of South Sudan—we thank you for being here—who I hope will convey our observations and great disappointment in the leadership to date as well as the importance of humanitarian access and sustained peace.

At this time, I will turn it over to our distinguished ranking member.

STATEMENT OF HON. BENJAMIN L. CARDIN, U.S. SENATOR FROM MARYLAND

Senator CARDIN. First, let me thank Senator Corker for convening this hearing on South Sudan.

South Sudan is pretty far from here. Most Americans probably could not find it on the map quickly, if at all. And the brutalities that are taking place there are of great concern to the world community, and it is important that we put a spotlight on it.

So, Mr. Chairman, I really do appreciate this hearing.

As you pointed out, in 2011, there was great hope for the newest nation in the world. But I must tell you today, I have never been more concerned whether this country will survive.

The circumstances there are extremely disappointing. As you point out, despite the August peace agreements, hostilities continue. People are being brutalized, young boys and girls, rape camps, the worst atrocities of modern times.

We all said after Darfur never again, and it is happening again. You pointed out that the United States has invested billions of dollars. And we have. We are concerned about stability in that part of the world, and we are prepared to be generous and invest resources for it to work.

But we are going to have to ask hard questions. And that is, looking at the returns, are these investments the best use of U.S. resources? We are going to have to ask hard questions, because this brutality just cannot continue.

There have been very difficult circumstances for people to try to do their work. The United Nations Deputy Special Representative on Humanitarian Coordination Toby Lanzer was expelled. Violence against aid workers is rising. And a troublesome draft bill governing the operation of nongovernmental organizations hangs over the head of humanitarian workers. How do we do work there?

While it is tempting to focus on the immediate call to support implementation of the peace agreement, we must also look at the long-term viability of South Sudan and how we engage with a government that engages in the types of abuses that have occurred.

So I have many questions today, starting with whether this peace agreement is viable. It does not look like either party is really serious about it. What do we plan to do if the parties' ceasefire violations and implementation delays continue? Are regional actors willing to maintain pressure on the parties to the conflict to monitor adherence to the agreement? And under what conditions should we and the international community be willing to support the government's recovery efforts, considering the parties' questionable commitment to the peace process, the level of official corruption, and what appears to be complete disinterest by those in power to commit to a development agenda that puts people of South Sudan first?

I want to be clear. I stand in support of the people of South Sudan. Their courage and resilience in the face of the abuse heaped upon them by the very people who are supposed to ensure their safety, security, and well-being is truly astonishing. I fully support life assistance programs that touch at the grassroots.

However, I remain skeptical about unconditional reconstruction packages. I am working on a proposal to condition some of the aid on a clear demonstration from South Sudan's Government that it will respect the terms of the peace agreement and ensure accountability of the egregious crimes committed in this conflict and that it will address corruption and invest in its own people. And I welcome my colleagues in joining me in this effort.

We must focus our attention on helping the innocents in South Sudan recover from the nightmare to which they have been subjected.

I look forward to hearing from our witnesses as to how we can achieve that objective.

The CHAIRMAN. Thank you. Thank you for those heartfelt comments.

Now, we will turn to our witnesses. On our first panel we will hear from two administration witnesses representing the State Department and USAID. The second panel consists of three informed experts on the situation in South Sudan.

Our first witness is Ambassador Donald Booth, the United States Special Envoy for Sudan and South Sudan since 2013.

Thank you for being here.

Our second witness is Bob Leavitt, the Deputy Assistant Administrator for USAID, the Bureau of Democracy at USAID Conflict and Humanitarian Assistance.

We want to thank you both for being here. I know you have testified before. If you can summarize in about 5 minutes, without objection, we will make your written testimony a part of the record. Then we obviously want to ask questions.

But if you would begin, Mr. Booth, we would appreciate it.

STATEMENT OF HON. DONALD BOOTH, SPECIAL ENVOY TO SUDAN AND SOUTH SUDAN, U.S. DEPARTMENT OF STATE, WASHINGTON, DC

AMBASSADOR BOOTH. Chairman Corker, Ranking Member Cardin, thank you for the opportunity to speak before you today.

The people of South Sudan have no greater friend than the United States. We stood with them, as you noted, during their long struggle for self-determination. We helped broker the comprehensive peace agreement and invested considerable resources in the run up to and following their independence.

But sadly, 2 years after independence, South Sudan's leaders decided to squander their country's future and far too many lives in a political power struggle.

Today, thanks in part to U.S. leadership and engagement, South Sudan does have a chance for a fresh start. It has the opportunity to close the door on conflict and reclaim the promise we saw at its birth.

I want to emphasize up front that the peace agreement signed in August, despite all the challenges of implementation since then, offers the best chance to put South Sudan back on the path to peace and development.

But the 2-year conflict created a devastating legacy: 2.4 million people facing severe, life-threatening hunger; 2.3 million South Sudanese displaced; and an economy in ruins. Violence persists in many parts of the country, and there are continued reports of heinous abuses of civilians.

Since the signing of the peace agreement, discussions over security arrangements for Juba and the opposition's return to the capital have become as complex and drawn-out as the peace negotiations themselves. We have heard negative rhetoric from the government directed at the United Nations and at countries like the United States that are working to support the people of South Sudan. And far too regularly, we have heard from both the government and the opposition that "we"—the United States and other donor countries—are the ones who must foot the bill for peace or else watch South Sudan return to war.

In response, our message has been clear and consistent: The United States has and will continue to support peace in South Sudan, but our funding for implementation will be commensurate with the seriousness of the commitment of both parties to realizing peace.

And I want to emphasize that the agreement would not have come about without the intensive diplomatic efforts of the United States. From helping convince the two parties to attend the peace negotiations mediated by the Intergovernmental Authority on Development (IGAD), to securing an expansion and change of mandate for the U.N. Mission in South Sudan, we were instrumental in those efforts.

When the parties signed a cessation of hostilities agreement in January 2014, we took the lead in creating the monitoring and verification mechanism. And when they kept fighting, the United States was in the lead of sanctioning those who were leading the fighting, initially bilaterally and then via the United Nations.

In May 2014, Secretary Kerry traveled to the region and helped convince President Kiir and opposition leader Machar to accept that a transitional government of national unity would be the way out of the conflict.

I spent much of 2014 and 2015 in the region, supporting the IGAD mediators and pressing the parties to compromise for peace and for the sake of the people of South Sudan.

In July of this year, President Obama met with regional leaders in Addis and helped forge the unity of purpose that was needed to convince the parties to sign the compromise peace agreement in August.

In October, Secretary Kerry met with the signatories together to reinforce our expectation that they adhere to the agreement for the good of their people.

Since the peace agreement was signed, implementation, unfortunately, has been slow and key deadlines have slipped. The central obstacle to implementation has been that the parties continue to see themselves as adversaries rather than as partners in a future transitional government.

But there has been progress. In early November, the government and opposition came to terms on security arrangements for Juba, and the opposition advance team is scheduled to travel to Juba in the next few days.

Ambassador Phee and our Embassy in Juba have played an important role in countering the misleading narratives of those who oppose the agreement and in building support for its implementation.

The Joint Monitoring and Evaluation Commission, or JMEC, the body that will oversee implementation of the agreement, has begun its work under the chairmanship of Festus Mogae, the former President of Botswana. He is a serious and capable leader.

And the parties have jointly committed in writing to form the transitional government of national unity in January.

South Sudan has a roadmap back to peace and stability because the peace agreement is as much about reform and healing as it is about power-sharing to end hostilities. Specifically, the peace agreement requires the transitional government to reform the security sector that dominated the state, to inject transparency into the public finances, to pursue reconciliation and accountability, to draft and obtain popular approval of a permanent constitution, and to hold elections.

True to our values, we intend to support transitional justice and the development of a robust civil society. We have already committed $5 million to that purpose.

We also intend to continue to support the South Sudanese people, especially the most vulnerable. You have noted the $1.3 billion of humanitarian assistance we have already provided.

In cooperation with other donors, we need to be prepared to support additional activities as implementation of the peace agreement proceeds, including priority areas such as security sector reform and reconstruction.

However, we will insist that the transitional government invest its own resources in these areas as well as provide ongoing transparent accounting of its public finances.

Our goal is to get South Sudan's leaders to seize this opportunity for peace and to stand up a transitional government.

Finally, South Sudan must close this chapter of conflict in order to pursue not only its own rebirth but to better improve relations with Sudan through resolution of the issues along their shared border, including that of the final status of Abyei. The internal strife in both countries has impeded resolution of these bilateral issues.

We remain engaged with the African Union's High-Level Implementation Panel and support its efforts to resolve the outstanding post-independence issues between Sudan and South Sudan, as well as the continuing conflicts inside Sudan in Darfur and the Two Areas.

Getting South Sudan's parties to implement the agreement, and bringing lasting peace to South Sudan, will require continued, intensive diplomatic effort. We are not naive. There are several ways this path can fail, and we would have to respond quickly in a manner consistent with any new reality.

But as I said earlier, the signed peace agreement, for all the challenges of implementation, currently offers the best chance for peace in South Sudan.

I thank you, Mr. Chairman, and members of the committee, for the opportunity to appear before you today. Thank you.

[The prepared statement of Ambassador Booth follows:]

PREPARED STATEMENT OF DONALD BOOTH

Chairman Corker, Ranking Member Cardin, and Members of the Committee, thank you for the opportunity to speak before you today.

The people of South Sudan have no greater friend than the United States. We stood with them during their long struggle for self-determination. We helped broker the Comprehensive Peace Agreement—or CPA—of 2005 and ensured that its provisions were respected. We invested considerable resources in the run up to and following South Sudan's independence in 2011. Sadly, two years after independence, South Sudan's leaders decided to squander their country's future and far too many lives in a political power struggle. Today, thanks in part to U.S. leadership and engagement, South Sudan has a chance for a fresh start. It has the opportunity to close the door on conflict and reclaim the promise we all saw at its birth as a nation four years ago.

I want to emphasize up front that the peace agreement signed in August, despite all the challenges of implementation since then, offers the best chance to put South Sudan back on the path to peace and development.

But the two year conflict created a devastating legacy: 2.4 million people facing severe, life-threatening hunger; 2.3 million South Sudanese displaced; and an economy in ruins. Violence persists in many parts of the country and there are continued reports of heinous abuses of civilians. Implementation of the peace agreement is behind schedule, and both sides bear responsibility for delays. The November deadline for establishing a Transitional Government of National Unity has slipped to January.

Since the signing of the agreement, we have too often heard the wrong messages from the government and the opposition. Both sides rush to accuse the other of violating the ceasefire or obstructing implementation—while themselves violating the ceasefire or obstructing implementation. We have watched discussions over security arrangements for Juba and the opposition's return to the capital become as complex and drawn-out as the peace negotiations themselves. We have heard negative rhetoric from the government directed at the United Nations, NGOs, journalists, civil society organizations, and at countries, like the United States, that are working to support the people of South Sudan. And far too regularly we have heard from both the government and the opposition that "we"—the United States and other donor countries—are the ones who must foot the bill for peace, or else watch South Sudan return to war.

In response, our message has been clear and consistent: the United States has and will continue to support peace in South Sudan. We are prepared to support implementation of the peace agreement, but our funding for implementation will be commensurate with the seriousness of the commitment of both parties to realizing peace.

And I want to emphasize that the agreement would not have come about without the intensive diplomatic efforts of the United States. We helped convince President Kiir and opposition leader Machar to send delegations to peace negotiations mediated by South Sudan's immediate neighbors and fellow members of the Intergovernmental Authority on Development—or IGAD. We secured the expansion of the U.N. Mission in South Sudan—or UNMISS—and refocused its mandate on protection of civilians, humanitarian assistance delivery and human rights monitoring.

When the parties signed a cessation of hostilities agreement in January 2014, we took the lead in organizing and funding the Monitoring and Verification Mechanism—or MVM—and when they kept fighting, we were the first to sanction those leading the fighting, first bilaterally and then through the United Nations with the backing of the international community. Secretary Kerry's May 2014 trip to Addis and Juba convinced President Kiir and opposition leader Machar to meet face to face and to accept a transitional government of national unity as the way out of conflict. I spent much of 2014 and 2015 in the region, supporting the IGAD mediators and pressing the parties to compromise for peace.

In July of this year, President Obama met with regional leaders in Addis and helped forge the unity of purpose that was needed to convince the parties to sign the compromise peace agreement in August. In October, Secretary Kerry met with the signatories to reinforce our expectation that they adhere to the agreement they signed and work together for the good of their people. Throughout the crisis we kept up a drumbeat of calls from senior Administration officials to South Sudanese and regional leaders to keep the peace process moving forward.

It has long been clear that no agreement was going to succeed without the active engagement of countries in the region through IGAD, particularly Uganda, Sudan, Kenya, and Ethiopia; and so it was crucial that any agreement be something the region could support. To bolster the IGAD process, the United States and other partners joined together as IGAD-Plus, to bring our collective leverage to bear as the region coalesced around an agreement amenable to all stakeholders. Maintaining our engagement with the region and other international partners will be vital to seeing the peace agreement implemented. The renewal next week of the UNMISS mandate will be an opportunity to further equip UNMISS to play a crucial role in supporting implementation of the agreement.

Since the peace agreement was signed, implementation has been slow and key deadlines have slipped. The central obstacle to implementation has been that the parties continue to see themselves as adversaries, rather than as partners in a future transitional government. But there has been progress. In early November, the government and opposition finally came to terms on security arrangements for Juba and other key towns. The advance team of opposition officials is scheduled to travel to Juba tomorrow. Ambassador Phee and our Embassy in Juba have played an important role in countering those in the government camp who opposed the agreement and in building grass roots support for the agreement's implementation. The Joint Monitoring and Evaluation Commission—or JMEC—the body that will oversee implementation of the agreement and act as an arbitrator between the parties when disagreements arise, has begun its work in Juba under the chairmanship of Festus Mogae, the former President of Botswana. He is a serious, capable leader. The parties jointly committed in writing to form the transitional government of national unity in January.

South Sudan has a roadmap back to peace and stability because the peace agreement is as much about reform and healing as it is about power sharing to end hostilities. Specifically, the peace agreement requires the transitional government to reform the security sector that dominated the state, to inject transparency in the public finances, to pursue reconciliation and accountability, to draft and obtain popular approval of a permanent constitution, and to hold elections under that new constitution.

Our immediate priority is to help establish the institutions needed to implement and oversee execution of the peace agreement. We are providing support to stand up the JMEC, perhaps the most critical institution in ensuring adherence to the agreement. We will also support a reformed and re-energized ceasefire monitoring mechanism—the Ceasefire and Transitional Security Arrangements Monitoring Mechanism, or CTSAMM—as well as the National Constitutional Amendment Commission and the Joint Operations Center.

True to our values, we intend to support transitional justice and the development of a robust civil society, including support for religious and women's groups. In May, Secretary Kerry committed $5 million toward supporting a credible, impartial, and effective mechanism to help end the cycle of impunity and vengeance that helped fuel the conflict. This funding could support the hybrid court that the parties committed in the peace agreement to create under the auspices of the African Union.

We also intend to continue to support the South Sudanese people, especially the most vulnerable groups, such as refugees and IDPs. The United States has been the single largest donor of humanitarian assistance for South Sudan, providing more than $1.3 billion since the start of the conflict.

In cooperation with other major donors, we need to be prepared to support additional activities as implementation proceeds, including priority areas such as security sector reform; disarmament, demobilization, and reintegration of former combatants; reconstruction of infrastructure in devastated urban centers like Bor, Bentiu, and Malakal; and reform of South Sudan's public financial management. However, we will insist that the transitional government invest its own resources in these areas as well as provide ongoing transparent accounting of its public finances.

The goal of our efforts is to get South Sudan's leaders to seize this opportunity for peace, and to stand up a transitional government capable of building the nation's institutions in order to provide basic services to its citizens. It must be ready to draft a new constitution; to heal the wounds of war through truth and reconciliation efforts and credible accountability mechanisms; and to build the country's economy and imposing rigor and transparency in its public financial management. And, finally, it must be ready to guide South Sudan to free and fair elections after three years.

We will continue to provide much-needed assistance to support these critical reforms. But let me be clear: our support for implementation will be proportional to the commitment of the South Sudanese leaders themselves. While we understand that it will take time for President Kiir and opposition leader Machar to rebuild enough trust to work together constructively, and for the transitional government to function as envisioned in the peace agreement, the government and the opposition must show that they are committed to this agreement, and to choosing peace over war, if we are to commit further U.S. resources.

Finally, South Sudan must close this chapter of conflict in order to pursue not only its own re-birth, but better relations with Sudan through resolution of the issues along their shared border, including the final status of Abyei. The internal strife in both countries has impeded resolution of these issues. We remain engaged with the African Union's High Level Implementation Panel (AU-HIP) and support its efforts to resolve the outstanding post-independence issues between Sudan and South Sudan as well as the continuing conflicts inside Sudan in Darfur and the "Two Areas" of Southern Kordofan and Blue Nile states.

Bringing the South Sudanese parties to the table required an intensive diplomatic effort. Getting the parties to implement the agreement, and bringing lasting peace to South Sudan, will require no less. Peace will be a process, not an event. It will require the sustained engagement and attention of the United States and the unity of purpose of IGAD, the African Union, and other key international partners. Moving South Sudan's leaders to take steps in implementing the August peace agreement, which is backed by the region and the international community, is the best way to start a virtuous cycle in which the parties to the conflict, as well as ordinary South Sudanese, begin to see the rewards of peace, and thus reduce their willingness to go back to war.

We are not naive; there are several ways this path can fail, and we would have to respond quickly in a manner consistent with any new reality. But, as I said earlier, the signed agreement, for all the challenges of implementation, currently offers the best chance for peace in South Sudan.

Thank you, Mr. Chairman and members of the committee, for the opportunity to speak and for your continued commitment to the people of South Sudan.

The CHAIRMAN. Thank you very much.

Mr. Leavitt?

STATEMENT OF BOB LEAVITT, DEPUTY ASSISTANT ADMINISTRATOR, BUREAU FOR DEMOCRACY, CONFLICT, AND HUMANITARIAN ASSISTANCE, U.S. AGENCY FOR INTERNATIONAL DEVELOPMENT, WASHINGTON, D.C.

Mr. LEAVITT. Chairman Corker, Ranking Member Cardin, and members of the committee, thank you for the opportunity to discuss the situation in South Sudan today, and thank you very much for your support.

Today, I would like to provide an update on the humanitarian situation, share how we are making a difference, and highlight how our programs assist the people of South Sudan.

As Special Envoy Booth has just highlighted, the peace agreement signed in August is the best chance for a return to peace and development. Its implementation is urgently needed.

The conflict in South Sudan has created a dire situation. Warring parties have brutalized civilians, perpetuating a cycle of violence and revenge. Women and children have been raped, killed, and burned alive. Over 2.3 million South Sudanese have fled their homes and lost everything.

Today, South Sudan is one of the most food-insecure countries in the world. Up to 2.4 million people in South Sudan, 20 percent of the population, face life-threatening hunger this month. The numbers will only increase in early 2016. People have resorted to eating water lilies and grass to survive.

Our partners face challenges reaching these people in need, especially in the hardest hit areas of the Greater Upper Nile Region.

Despite these challenges, though, we are doing everything possible with our diplomatic colleagues to save lives. The United States is the largest donor to the people of South Sudan, providing $1.3 billion in humanitarian assistance. Our staff and partners have helped avert famine for 2 consecutive years.

In October, I saw firsthand how we are making a difference on the ground. Several colleagues and I flew by helicopter from government-controlled Malakal to opposition-controlled Wau Shilluk, a remote area in the Greater Upper Nile Region. Hundreds of South Sudanese greeted us as we landed.

Several months before then, these very people were nearly inaccessible due to conflict. It was humbling to meet such incredibly resilient people.

It was also at the same time inspiring to see our staff, our partners, do whatever it takes to reach such people in need. But it was also disappointing that we must continue to rely on such complex air operations to get that job done. It was there that we saw three large air operations at that time.

Every day, aid workers, 90 percent of whom are South Sudanese, are saving lives. They endure daily obstacles to reach people. Warring parties have assaulted and killed aid workers and interfered with the delivery of humanitarian assistance for the people.

USAID staff and our partners are relentless, constantly innovating to reach people as safely and efficiently as possible. They deploy teams with lightweight packs to deliver assistance. They use canoes. They use tractors to navigate tributaries and swamps. They find new routes to get to people in need.

Thanks to their efforts, we reach 1.28 million people with our assistance, and that is the story behind the $1.3 billion figure. We provide them with food, water, health care, and trauma support. We have also shifted our long-term assistance to more directly meet the needs of the people of South Sudan.

As over 400,000 children have lost access to school during this crisis, we have moved our education program to provide emergency education, standing up 629 emergency learning spaces in the country, enrolling 130,000 children who are in them, including children demobilized from armed conflicts. Providing an opportunity for education demonstrates our commitment as the American people to the people of South Sudan and to its next generation.

We have helped protect civilians, especially women and children. We empower women to make informed decisions so they can access water, hygiene, and other needs safely. We have helped bolster civil society and expand access to independent radio in eight states in the country to better inform South Sudanese about the status of the peace agreement and its implementation.

In achieving these results, we have worked closely with donor, NGO, and U.N. partners, including the U.N. Peacekeeping Mission in South Sudan that continues to save lives daily. We appreciate the support of our diplomatic colleagues, both here in Washington and in Juba. We also appreciate our committed USAID staff both in Washington and in the field.

For decades, successive administrations, the U.S. Congress, and the American people have stood by the people of South Sudan. We remain committed to working with the people of South Sudan through this difficult situation, but this is a critical time as they move along the path to peace.

For our assistance to be most effective, all parties must allow unfettered access to aid workers to reach those in need, wherever they may be.

However, no amount of assistance will end the suffering. Only peace will.

Thank you for your time, and I look forward to your questions.

[The prepared statement of Mr. Leavitt follows:]

PREPARED STATEMENT OF BOB LEAVITT

Introduction

Chairman Corker, Ranking Member Cardin, and Members of the Committee, thank you for the opportunity to discuss the situation in South Sudan, and for your continued support.

Today, I would like to provide an update of the situation on the ground, share how we are making a difference and saving lives, and highlight how we have adapted our programs to help the people of South Sudan achieve a lasting peace.

Situational update

Two years of conflict in South Sudan has created a devastating humanitarian crisis. The peace agreement signed in August provides the best chance for a return to peace and development. Its implementation is urgently needed. The people of South Sudan are suffering and the humanitarian situation is only getting worse. Response teams cannot reach people who need aid the most, especially in the Greater Upper Nile Region, due to local clashes and authorities denying access.

Civilians have borne the brunt of the violence since the conflict erupted in December 2013. Warring parties have failed to protect civilians. Warring parties have reportedly killed and brutalized unarmed civilians, perpetuating cycles of retribution and exacting reprehensible cruelty. The African Union Commission of Inquiry and human rights organizations have documented flagrant atrocities. Several United Nations (UN) reports recount allegations that warring parties gang-raped and burned women and children alive in their homes; castrated, raped, and killed children; and forcibly recruited as many as 16,000 children. These allegations demand a full and impartial accounting as implementation of the peace agreement moves forward.

More than 2.3 million South Sudanese have fled their homes in search of safety and protection, since December 2013. Almost one third—nearly 655,000 people—fled to Ethiopia, Sudan, Uganda, and Kenya. Combined with refugees who had fled before the crisis, a total of 770,000 South Sudanese refugees are now unable to return home. These countries generously support South Sudanese refugees in the midst of other stresses, including the El Nino-related drought in Ethiopia.

Two thirds of those displaced by this conflict—1.7 million people—remain internally displaced in South Sudan, mostly in remote areas. Others have sought refuge in protection of civilians sites that were established on the bases of the U.N. Mission in the Republic of South Sudan (UNMISS). Two weeks after the crisis began, 60,000 people were sheltered there.

Two years later, approximately 185,000 people remain in overcrowded protection of civilians sites on six UNMISS bases. The Bentiu and Malakal sites more than doubled their population this year. We applaud UNMISS for receiving and protecting civilians on its bases. This unprecedented act saved lives. The untenable situation at these sites underscores the urgency of all parties to stop fighting, create stable and secure conditions, and resume essential services so that civilians can return home safely. As of now, displaced persons remain fearful of returning home. The U.S. Government will support informed, voluntary returns or relocation only when it becomes feasible and safe to do so.

Up to 2.4 million people in South Sudan—or 20 percent of the population—face life-threatening hunger this month. This figure is 60 percent higher than last December. It will increase to 2.6 million and higher in early 2016 as the limited harvest runs out. In fact, today, South Sudan is one of the most food-insecure countries in the world. People have resorted to eating water lilies and grass to survive in remote areas. A quarter of a million children suffer from severe acute malnutrition. The situation could become worse without immediate and consistent access for aid groups.

The warring parties have set back development gains. According to UNICEF, 57 percent of government health facilities have been destroyed or are not operational in the Greater Upper Nile Region (Unity, Upper Nile, and Jonglei states). More than 800 schools have been destroyed during the conflict. Over 400,000 children have lost access to schools, bringing the total number of children out of school to 1.8 million.

The economy is in a state of near collapse. Food, safe drinking water, and other basic goods are less available and less affordable due to rising inflation and currency depreciation. Across the country, food prices are up to 150 percent above average. The cost of fuel is also up, which makes delivery of assistance more expensive.

Access challenges

Our teams and partners are doing everything possible to reach those in need with assistance. The operating environment remains challenging and risky. Humanitarian workers face daily security, logistical, and bureaucratic impediments, especially in the Greater Upper Nile Region.

Warring parties continue to target humanitarian staff. Since the conflict began, at least 40 humanitarian workers have lost their lives. In October of this year alone, the U.N. documented more than 78 incidents nationwide in which warring parties looted supplies, robbed offices, assaulted aid workers, or interfered with aid operations. In June, the government expelled the UN's top humanitarian official. This incident brought attention to the challenges all of our partners are facing, but it is important to note that most of the aid workers under attack are South Sudanese. More than 90 percent of aid workers in non-governmental organizations (NGOs) are South Sudanese who risk their own lives to help fellow citizens.

Warring parties complicate aid delivery in what is already a tough place to operate. South Sudan has very little infrastructure, and rain makes large parts of the country inaccessible by road for months at a time. Bad roads are made worse by criminals who harass aid trucks.

Thus, our partners often rely on river barges to deliver aid. When government and opposition forces ramped up fighting in April and May, the barges were caught in the crossfire, disrupting their passage to Unity, Upper Nile, and Jonglei states. In July, the government closed off the Nile River entirely. To reach people around Malakal, the largest city in that area, our partners resorted to air operations, which are five times more expensive than delivery by barge.

Our partners also face bureaucratic impediments. The government has repeatedly refused requests from impartial humanitarian organizations to airlift food or other critical relief aid to people in need. Aid workers must spend precious time that should be used reaching people, haggling with military and political leaders from all sides over access. South Sudanese authorities have denied visas for aid workers, denied delivery of cash or equipment to opposition-held areas, and charged exorbitant fees for the registration of NGOs.

These restrictions are unacceptable under any circumstances, but they are especially taxing at a time when our humanitarian dollars and operations are stretched thin by an unprecedented number of protracted crises around the world.

U.S. response

Notwithstanding immense challenges, the United States is leading the effort to help the people of South Sudan through these tough times. The U.S. government is the largest donor to the response for the South Sudan humanitarian crisis. We have provided more than $1.3 billion in emergency assistance for conflict-affected people in South Sudan and South Sudanese refugees in the region since the start of the crisis. We also work closely with other donors to speak with one voice and coordinate our responses to needs, including being sensitive to conflict dynamics and ensuring our activities do not inadvertently intensify or trigger additional tensions.

In late October, I saw firsthand how we are making a difference. Several UN, donor, and Department of State colleagues and I flew by helicopter from government-controlled Malakal to opposition-controlled Wau Shilluk, a remote area across the river in the Greater Upper Nile Region. We saw our partners, including the U.N. World Food Programme (WFP), World Vision, and others, providing assistance in an area that they could not reach earlier. As we met community groups, it was humbling to be with such incredibly resilient people. As we met aid workers and watched three large air deliveries of food, it was inspiring to see their resolve to do whatever it takes to save lives. It is also disappointing that we must resort to such complex measures to help those in need.

We are working as effectively and efficiently as possible by leveraging the expertise of our partners. Drawing on experiences from around the world, they are using creative tactics to reach people who would otherwise be cut off from aid. For example, one USAID partner reached remote displaced populations in Upper Nile State by navigating river tributaries and using tractors to cross swampy terrain. WFP has expanded road routes to adapt and reroute when violence or other obstacles get in the way. WFP has found new places to land in support of air operations. WFP also works with the governments of Sudan, Ethiopia, Kenya, and Uganda to bring aid across each of their borders to maximize efficiency. UNICEF and partners have reached over 880,000 people—a quarter of whom are children under age five—by deploying mobile teams to quickly deliver aid in hard-to-reach areas. Food for the Hungry has used canoes and an extensive community network to distribute seeds to communities in need.

Our partners are improving the everyday lives of people in South Sudan. We reach approximately 1.3 million people per month with food, clean water, health care, and trauma support. For two consecutive years, U.S. government assistance has helped avert famine and supported communities that would otherwise be at greater risk. We have encouraged and supported Ethiopia, Kenya, Sudan, and Uganda in keeping their borders open to receive and host South Sudanese refugees. Yet, with 2.4 million people facing severe hunger each month, and humanitarian appeals significantly underfunded, more needs to be done.

Adapting our response to support peace

We are doing all we can, but we are deeply disappointed that the government is not acting in the best interest of its people. It is clear that we must match our steadfast goodwill toward the people of South Sudan with demands for accountability by the government and all parties. They must stop harassing aid workers and NGOs, grant full, unhindered humanitarian access, and take credible steps towards peace.

USAID has shifted its long-term assistance from helping to build the institutions of the new South Sudanese state to more directly meeting the needs of the South Sudanese people. We have withdrawn all technical advisors we previously provided to government ministries, with the exception of the Ministry of Health, where our advisors are needed to support life-saving programs and avoid the spread of disease. We have expanded support to protect and empower women, educate children, safeguard civil society, and support independent media.

Supporting women

We are protecting civilians at risk of violence, especially women and children who have suffered unspeakable brutality at the hands of armed actors. For instance, at the protection of civilians site in Malakal, USAID provided lighting around the site's perimeter to increase safety and visibility for women and girls who can be at risk of sexual violence after dark. We also support seven partners across South Sudan to reduce the risk of Gender-Based Violence (GBV) and provide survivors with safe spaces and clinical and trauma care. They have reached 950,000 people with information on GBV prevention and response in 2015. We also integrate GBV prevention in all programs. For example, in water, sanitation, and hygiene programs, we empower women to inform decisions that will make it safer for women to access water facilities.

We are also providing women with opportunities to make a living and keep their families healthy. Our assistance has helped women like Nyakuoth, a widow with five children whose husband was killed when fighting broke out in her village this past May. Nyakuoth and her children lived in the bush for three months, eating wild leaves to survive. Thanks to our medical care and therapeutic foods, she was able to revive her malnourished children. We also provided her with seeds that she is saving for a peaceful harvest. "I pray for peace to return," she told our partner, "so that we can go back home and plant crops to feed [my] children."

Educating children

If South Sudan is to have a peaceful future, we must create opportunities for the next generation. In partnership with UNICEF, USAID is providing emergency education services to internally displaced children, including those in protection of civilians sites and opposition-held areas. The program has established 629 temporary learning spaces across six states (Lakes, Unity, Jonglei, Upper Nile, Central Equatoria, and Eastern Equatoria). We have enrolled nearly 130,000 children and adolescents, including recently demobilized child soldiers. USAID partners have also helped to reunite nearly 2,400 children with their families.

We have also helped equip a new cadre of female educators. Fourteen women scholars returned to South Sudan over the summer after earning Master's degrees in Education in Emergencies at Indiana University. An ethnically diverse group selected from across South Sudan, they are now equipped to teach tolerance and understanding among South Sudan's diverse communities.

Supporting civil society and independent media

South Sudanese civil society and media play a pivotal watchdog role, but they face an increasingly difficult operating environment that includes legal impediments, security threats, and hostile statements from the government. We are working to prevent the closing space for civil society organizations by ramping up support to improve their operational security and advocacy skills. We are especially concerned about a bill under consideration in South Sudan's National Legislative Assembly that could negatively impact civil society and our humanitarian partners. We have engaged the government to revise elements of the bill, but encourage the Assembly to allow for greater consultation and feedback from civil society on this legislation. We are also deeply concerned about a new National Security law that gives sweeping powers to the National Security Service to arrest and detain activists and journalists.

To advance the formal peace process, we are supporting civil society groups and independent media channels so that they can inform the South Sudanese public about the peace agreement and its implementation. We support community consultations where partners distribute copies of the agreement, translate it into local languages, and discuss how it might impact these communities. We also support independent radio, the primary means of reaching people in South Sudan; the radio stations we assist reach millions of listeners.

Conclusion

The U.S. government remains committed to saving the lives and aspirations of the people of South Sudan. However, no amount of assistance will end the suffering; only peace will. We remain concerned that ongoing clashes continue to make it challenging, or even impossible, for people to receive desperately needed aid or to resume their lives in some of the hardest hit areas. Both sides must show a credible and unequivocal commitment to implement all elements of the August peace agreement without delay.

All warring parties are required by international humanitarian principles to ensure impartial humanitarian access to people in need across conflict lines throughout all of South Sudan.

Through concerted diplomacy, we must continue to push to ensure all parties respect this most basic principle. We greatly appreciate the work of our Department of State colleagues both here in Washington and in the field to urge respect for these principles. All humanitarian staff—from top U.N. officials to truck drivers delivering lifesaving food—must be free to carry out their work free from violence or retribution. Harassing those who are saving lives in South Sudan ultimately punishes the vulnerable and traumatized people who need them most.

Working hand-in-hand with the people of South Sudan to save lives in difficult circumstances has created strong bonds among aid workers. While in Juba recently, I saw the extent to which members of the humanitarian community look out for each other. A USAID colleague came to a high-level meeting with a backpack full of high protein bars and supplies—a care package bought at her own expense—for NGO partners who had staff preparing to travel through swamps and difficult terrain to deliver aid. Their solidarity runs deep.

The commitment of our partners and the resilience of the South Sudanese inspire us. Our commitment to the people of South Sudan makes a difference, saving lives and setting a path to the future. The people of South Sudan deserve to live in communities free from harm. It is with these men and women in mind that we remain steadfast in advancing USAID's mission to partner to end extreme poverty and promote resilient, democratic societies while advancing our security and prosperity.

The CHAIRMAN. Thank you both for your testimony. It is disheartening, at a minimum.

So, Mr. Leavitt, you talked about all the challenges that we have in delivering aid. I certainly appreciate some of the examples that you gave. But from what we understand, the United Nations and humanitarian partner organizations have been specifically targeted by government and proxy forces, including the apparent targeting of senior officials and humanitarians delivering to millions displaced by atrocity.

So how do we push back against such impunity toward this humanitarian imperative? How do we do that? I mean, I would assume that, in some ways, the aid that we are providing is actually helping these government officials, is it not?

Mr. LEAVITT. Thank you very much for the question. We very much share your concern. We are, of course, very much concerned about the safety of aid workers.

The CHAIRMAN. Let me just, specifically, are government officials targeting them?

Mr. LEAVITT. The rhetoric has not been positive in South Sudan. There has not been a positive rhetoric that accepts that aid workers are there to help. There has not been the message that well over 90 percent of all aid workers are South Sudanese, many of whom are putting themselves at risk to help the people——

The CHAIRMAN. So are government officials and/or proxies targeting people delivering humanitarian aid?

Mr. LEAVITT. The aid workers have been affected by both parties, yes, sir, government and opposition forces.

The CHAIRMAN. We have people here from the Embassy of South Sudan. I would just say you ought to be embarrassed. I do not know how you can come to the hearing like this, representing the Government of South Sudan, knowing that we have expended $1.3 billion on behalf of the people that you represent and you are targeting aid workers. I would be embarrassed to be at a hearing like this.

I would be embarrassed to send out the kind of press release that you sent out prior to this hearing.

I do not know what kind of government you represent.

Let me ask you this. Does the aid that we provide help in any way stabilize the government that is there?

Mr. LEAVITT. Our assistance goes to the people of South Sudan. Since this conflict began, our humanitarian assistance goes directly, in tandem with our partners, the U.N. and nongovernmental organizations, goes directly in support of the people of South Sudan.

Our long-term assistance at one point was working in support of the government ministries as they were established in 2011. We have since changed that assistance since 2013 and early 2014, changed it to support programs that go directly to the people.

So just as an example, we used to provide support through advisers in the Ministry of Education to help build up that ministry. But as a result of the outbreak of conflict, we have shifted that assistance to emergency learning centers, in tandem with our partner UNICEF, so that assistance with the U.N. goes directly to the people and not with and in support of the ministry.

The CHAIRMAN. Mr. Booth, thank you for your efforts relative to the peace agreement. We all know how difficult the situation is there.

I would just ask both of you, since this agreement has been reached in August, has there been any greater access relative to humanitarian assistance or is it pretty much the same?

AMBASSADOR BOOTH. Mr. Chairman, let me give you one example of the efforts that our Embassy in Juba has made that has resulted in an increase.

Our Ambassador engaged directly with the Governor of Unity State, which has been the scene of much of the fighting that has continued since the signing of the peace agreement, and was able to achieve agreement to allow both humanitarian workers and the U.N. mission to send some of its troops into Leer in Unity State to access populations that in the past have been denied.

We have been working on the ground in South Sudan. There are many other examples of where our Embassy and our AID colleagues there have been out in the field pushing the envelope.

Mr. Leavitt mentioned the trip that he did where they were able to cross lines in Upper Nile State from government-controlled Malakal across the Nile River into the opposition-controlled areas. That effort resulted in greater access to people who had been in dire need.

But we are not able to reach everybody. There continues to be harassment of aid workers, of assistance delivery.

The CHAIRMAN. By government officials and/or their proxies?

AMBASSADOR BOOTH. I think it is at a more retail level. It is not an official policy that has been pursued. But as Mr. Leavitt said, the negative rhetoric about the U.N. mission has contributed to a sense that you can attack these people with impunity.

We have urged that the rhetoric be changed, that the U.N. and those providing assistance be recognized as helping the people of South Sudan. We continue to push both government and opposition on access and on getting to a more positive rhetoric, so that aid workers are in less danger.

The CHAIRMAN. Let me ask you this. Have government officials in any way helped escort the United Nations personnel and/or others that are delivering through canoes and doing the other kind of things that have occurred? Has there been any assistance by the government itself to ensure that this aid reaches people who are in such need?

AMBASSADOR BOOTH. The problem, in general, has come where the government says, "We cannot guarantee your security if you go to this location." Or the opposition says, "We cannot guarantee your security if you go to that location."

So this game has been played to try to discourage delivery of assistance to areas that are on the other side. Again, we continue to push very strongly. "We are not asking for your guarantees. The U.N. is not asking for your guarantees. What we are asking is simply that you give us the assurance that they will be safe in areas you control."

In general, we have gotten cooperation in that regard. But there is the area in between, and there is a lot of retail freelancing that goes on that makes this a very difficult problem to get on top of.

The CHAIRMAN. Thank you, both.

Senator Cardin?

Senator CARDIN. Thank you, Mr. Chairman.

My children's generation grew up with Darfur as their battle call for international humanity. They got engaged in that campaign because of the brutalities that were taking place in Darfur. They said never again. It is happening again.

A peace agreement is the best option, if it is viable. The ceasefire has not been adhered to. People are being brutalized. The target date for the coalition government has come and passed, and there is no coalition government.

What is plan B, in order to protect the people of South Sudan? Does the international community with U.S. leadership have a plan B, so we are not faced with a growing and longstanding endangerment of the people of South Sudan, as we saw in Darfur?

AMBASSADOR BOOTH. Thank you very much, Senator, for that question. It really is at the crux of what we grapple with every day, how to move this peace agreement forward so that the fighting really does stop and this brutality does stop.

Again, our engagement with the parties has been consistent. As I noted, there has been progress.

I think one of the key things in moving toward the establishment of the transitional government will be the return of opposition delegation to Juba, which is expected literally within the next few days. Our Ambassador just had a meeting today in Juba with both government and opposition to work out some of the details of this.

That will be a very important event. With the opposition sitting in Juba, it will be much easier for President Mogae and the joint monitoring commission and the other mechanisms foreseen in the peace agreement to operate and for some of these mechanisms, such as the joint military command center to oversee the ceasefire, that that will be up and running. So far, the opposition has not had people there to participate in those.

I think this will be a fundamental change.

But if this does not move forward, and I think the critical thing is, it is a little bit dangerous to start talking about plan Bs, because they tend to undermine what you are trying to push forward, which is implementation of this peace agreement.

But clearly, one of the things that we have done is we have change the mandate of UNMISS to focus on protection of civilians. We are now in New York. By the 15th of this month, we will be renewing that mandate and are supporting the request of UNMISS for additional troops and police in order to expand this protection mission and also to enable UNMISS to be supportive of the peace agreement.

Senator CARDIN. I want to follow up on that. But first, I join the chairman and thank you for your leadership, I also thank the United States for what we are doing, as well as our international partners and the United Nations, for what they are doing. It is a very tough environment. We understand that, and we appreciate the great personal sacrifices that the people on the ground in South Sudan are making in order to save lives. They have our strong support, let me make no mistake about that.

But I would give you my assessment. I think Congress will pass a plan B, it is a matter of when, if the peace process does not go forward. I am not sure what that plan B is going to be. I do not want to undermine the peace process, but we will not tolerate the status quo. We just will not.

So I just urge us to have a very candid discussion of the realities on the ground and what actions we can take to protect the population.

Yes, the United Nations has been effective. As I understand it, they have several protected sites. A couple hundred thousand are protected. There is a much larger population that is not protected.

What do we do about that population? Increase the size of the U.N. mission? Fine. But there are still going to be hundreds of thousands at risk. If the peace process does not move forward, what do we do to protect those hundreds of thousands? And what do we do to hold those who have committed these atrocities accountable?

AMBASSADOR BOOTH. Well, accountability is one of the issues that we, in the process of negotiations of the peace agreement, fought very hard to keep front and center. There is an agreement of the parties that not only should there be truth, healing, and reconciliation, but there should also be accountability. And the parties have agreed to the establishment of a hybrid court under the African Union.

I also want to mention within a week of the outbreak of the conflict, within 2 weeks of the outbreak of the conflict, the African Union held a summit of its Peace and Security Council and established a Commission of Inquiry, which was headed by former Nigerian President Obasanjo. And the report that he and his team have compiled and the fact that the A.U. has now released that report I think sends a very strong signal that their African neighbors, not just the broader international community but Africa itself, is focused on ensuring that there is accountability for the atrocities that have occurred and is sending a signal to try to prevent those in the future.

Senator CARDIN. Secretary Kerry announced $5 million in support, I believe, of the accountability initiative. So what is the status of the establishment of the hybrid court? Do you envision that there will be a need for direct U.S. support for the hybrid court? Or international community support for the hybrid court? How do you see going after at the highest levels those who are responsible for the atrocities that have been committed?

AMBASSADOR BOOTH. If I recall the peace agreement correctly, I think the hybrid court, the deadline for establishing that is toward the end, November or December, of 2016. We have been engaging the African Union, which is responsible for establishing that court, and encouraging them to continue to move forward.

We have also started our own effort for documentation, collecting documentation for events that have happened, so that South Sudanese can get on the record what has happened. This information collected by the U.N. panel of experts, by UNMISS, by the monitoring and verification mechanism, all of these will be fed into this hybrid court.

Senator CARDIN. Let me make this observation. I had a conversation with Ambassador Power here yesterday. She was in your seat before this committee on U.N. peacekeeping.

Being held accountable for atrocities and violations of international standards is not a matter between the two political sides of South Sudan. There is an international interest that those responsible are held accountable. It is not left up to the parties. We prefer the country to take care of it itself. If it cannot, then the international community must respond.

Do we have your commitment that the United States will carry out its traditional role of making sure there is an effective accountability institution established so that the people of South Sudan know the perpetrators will be brought to justice?

AMBASSADOR BOOTH. I can assure you, Senator, that we very much are committed to seeing that there will be not only reconciliation but accountability. We believe that accountability is going to be critical to ensuring or at least diminishing the chances that there is repetition of what has happened in South Sudan. We believe we need to give the African Union the opportunity to form this hybrid court and that we should support it. And yes, we probably will be coming to seek funding to support that effort. And we will continue to push them to move forward as quickly as possible.

Senator CARDIN. So do not take this personally, because I very much respect the work you are doing—I mean that—and your commitment to justice. That is sincere.

I just wish our diplomats would be clearer on this issue. You give too much of a diplomatic response. The answer is that the United States needs to exercise strong international leadership that the perpetrators of these atrocities will be held accountable, period, the end. We will use every means we can so that never again means never again.

Thank you.

The CHAIRMAN. Just out of curiosity, before we move to the next panel, just by virtue of acknowledging what Senator Cardin just said, would it not mean that with any standard court, both the leader and the former vice president would end up in jail very soon? I am just curious. I mean, it sounds to me like incredible atrocities are being created and done by both of them and their proxies. Would not any standard court mean that both these folks that we are dealing with will end up in jail very soon? I am just curious.

AMBASSADOR BOOTH. Well, I think that is a decision that has to be made by a competent judicial authority, the hybrid court being the one that has been agreed upon for dealing with this in South Sudan. Clearly, the African Union Commission of Inquiry report has pointed in the direction of responsibility from the highest levels.

The CHAIRMAN. So we are basically negotiating with people that we assume are going to be in jail very soon. Is that correct?

AMBASSADOR BOOTH. Well, that has been the great conundrum of this and many other conflicts, that the people who are fighting are the ones that you have to get to negotiate.

But as I said in my testimony, the peace agreement is about more than just power-sharing to stop the fighting. It is about a program for reform, which they have committed to undertake and to which the international community will be holding them responsible.

That is why the JMEC, the Joint Monitoring and Evaluation Commission, was created under the peace agreement and is headed by a former president, a respected president in Africa. We are a member of that committee. And we, indeed, will be ensuring that the reform element of the peace agreement and the accountability elements are carried out, as well as just the power-sharing.

Thank you.

The CHAIRMAN. Listen, we thank you both for being here. I think, especially as a result of this hearing, but because of the atrocities that are occurring, I think you are going to find both of us pursuing these judicial issues that you are referring to.

Again, I do not know how representatives from South Sudan can show up at these types of meetings without being totally embarrassed by the actions of the government. I know we probably do not have representatives from the opposition here.

But we thank you both for your work and certainly are very despondent over what is occurring there at present.

Thank you.

Senator CARDIN. Mr. Leavitt, if there is anything we can do in regards to more effective delivery of humanitarian assistance, please let us know.

The CHAIRMAN. Thank you.

So we will now move to our second panel. We again thank you for the service of both of you and hopefully we have helped you in some way this morning.

All right, we thank you for being here.

Our first witness will be Ambassador Princeton Lyman. He has been here before. He is a former U.S. Special Representative for Sudan and South Sudan and currently the senior adviser to the president of the U.S. Institute of Peace.

We thank you very much for being here. I enjoyed seeing you recently.

The second witness will be John Prendergast, someone we see often, the founding director of the ENOUGH Project and former National Security Staff Adviser for African Affairs.

Thank you so much.

Our third witness will be Adotei Akwei, managing director of the government relations for Amnesty International.

We thank you for your service to the world.

If you all could summarize your comments in about 5 minutes, we look forward to questions. Again, thank you all for being here.

If you would just start and go in order, that would be good. Thank you.

STATEMENT OF HON. PRINCETON LYMAN, SENIOR ADVISOR TO THE PRESIDENT, FORMER SPECIAL ENVOY TO SUDAN AND SOUTH SUDAN, U.S. INSTITUTE OF PEACE, WASHINGTON, DC

Ambassador LYMAN. Thank you very much, Mr. Chairman. Thank you for holding this hearing. I appreciate that the full testimony can be put in the record.

You have heard already about the scope of this tragedy. I will not go into more detail. But the situation on the ground is, in fact, very grim. Fighting continues. Atrocities are being carried out. Some of the fighting has extended into new areas like Western Equatoria.

I would like to do several things here. I would like to address some of the questions you and Senator Cardin have raised, specifically the validity and fragility of the present peace agreement, questions of justice and accountability, and a plan B, if necessary.

First, let me just mention, we have a long history in the United States, bipartisan, of being involved and engaged in problems in Sudan, starting with President George W. Bush's selection of former Senator John Danforth as a special envoy, playing a major role in the comprehensive peace agreement. That has continued on with President Obama, appointments like Ambassador Booth and the actions of President Obama and Secretary Kerry.

We have done this over the years because problems in Sudan and South Sudan affect the security of a very sensitive region in Africa and the Red Sea area, which is the Horn of Africa, and we are concerned about the people who have suffered under these wars.

The security consideration continues today. So does the moral consideration.

I can understand the despair and even the anger in having to deal with this situation when so much has been squandered, but I think we have a commitment and a need to do whatever we can to address it.

Now, the African countries have traditionally been in the lead in these negotiations, and rightfully so, because they are affected most directly. And if you put any major sanctions on, like an arms embargo or trade embargo, they have to enforce it.

IGAD, the neighboring countries under the Intergovernmental Authority on Development, have been leading this peace process. But they have been divided. Sudan and Uganda are rivals for influence in this area, carrying on almost a proxy war in South Sudan. Ethiopia and Kenya have had their disagreements. People in all these countries are involved in one way or another in the arms trade or economic activities.

Although IGAD has frequently suggested that it would recommend an arms embargo or tougher sanctions, it has never done so, and because it does not do so, it is impossible for the Security Council to impose an embargo and sanctions and hope that such things will be enforced. So African unity is important.

Now, IGAD has accomplished a lot. As Ambassador Booth pointed out, a peace agreement has been painstakingly put together. But it is fragile, and it is fragile for several reasons.

One, as has been noted, it relies heavily on the actions and cooperation of the two people who are leading the war, President Kiir and former vice president Riek Machar.

Second, the security arrangements that are involved—that is, each side brings forces into Juba to protect themselves and each other—is not a prescription for security and safety.

Third, there has to be much more international involvement in making this agreement work. So let me speak to what I think are three things that need to be done by the Africans, by the U.N., and by the United States to help make this agreement work.

First, on the part of the Africans, they have appointed, as has been pointed out, a very distinguished African leader, Festus Moghae, to head of the Joint Monitoring and Evaluation Committee overseeing this agreement. But he should be given the powers of a high commissioner. He should have the powers to call the parties to order, to veto appointments that make no sense, make appointments of his own, take control over the budgetary and economic aspects of the government, and recommend to IGAD and to the African Union and the Security Council further sanctions if the parties do not carry these things forward.

Second, the hybrid court, no, not the end of 2016. The head of the hybrid court should be appointed now because working hand in glove with Festus Moghae, that is where you put pressure on the parties to move forward under this agreement.

Third, I think on the security arrangements, either an enhanced UNMISS or a special African Union force has to be added to the mix, if there is going to be security in Juba or in the other major cities to make this system work.

Now on the part of the United Nations, Senator Corker, you are absolutely right to press for who is attacking the U.N. and undermining it. I find it shocking that the Government of South Sudan has for a long time spoken against UNMISS, denigrated its work. And we know that patrols going out, brave patrols going out, are being shot at by various entities.

The Sanctions Committee of the U.N. has launched an investigation of who is blocking the peace process. The final report of that committee is going to the U.N. probably this month to be examined by the Security Council, hopefully made public. And I hope it will provide the answers that you asked for as to exactly who is doing this, who is responsible for attacks.

I would add that when the U.N. renews UNMISS this month, it should make clear again that attacks on U.N. peacekeepers is a war crime and those responsible will be pursued and made accountable.

I would like to see that same legal precedent for attacks on aid workers. Forty-one aid workers have been killed in South Sudan. That too requires accountability.

Getting the hybrid court up is good and important, but the U.N. has a responsibility as well.

Let me turn to the United States and the work that Ambassador Booth and the administration are doing; it is terrific, but it takes more push. President Obama did a very important thing when he was in Addis, I think it was in July. He called the parties together. He called the IGAD heads of state together and said: We need more urgency in this process. The U.S. is prepared to go ahead with its own sanctions. We are prepared to take other steps.

That helped inject urgency and it led, I think in large part, to the final signing of the peace agreement. But the peace agreement lags. It is fragile. It is in trouble.

At the next meeting that IGAD holds with its international partners, I would like to see Vice President Joe Biden go and inject the same sense of urgency that these parties must move forward, for additional steps made to strengthen the international role, and make it happen.

Finally, let me get to Senator Cardin's question about plan B. Let me first talk about other things I want the U.S. to do, and I know the U.S. is already doing some of these.

Peace agreements necessarily in the end involve bringing the guys with the guns to the table, but peace agreements do not last if they rest on that alone. Now, on paper, this is a very comprehensive peace agreement. It calls for a new constitution. It calls for economic reform. It calls for a lot of things.

But those two leaders are not committed to those actions. So you have to bring in civil society. You have to bring in women's groups. You have to bring in other professionals. And the United States can lend very strong support in this peace process to their participation, and insist upon it.

Now let me turn to plan B, if this fails. I think the only way then thereafter is to raise this problem to a much higher level, to having a meeting at the U.N. of relevant heads of state, and I would see the United States playing a major role, which comes to an agreement with all the major countries involved on several steps, an arms embargo, a trade embargo on anything except food and medicine. Let us starve the fighting, not the people. Let us make sure that all the other mechanisms of accountability are set up. And then the Africans must commit to enforcing those bans all along their border. Then you have a joint U.N.-A.U. mediator move forward together on a new, more comprehensive process.

This is the only way, it seems to me, raising it to a much higher level, taking much tougher steps on the parties, if this current agreement does not succeed.

Thank you very much. I am sorry to go over on my time.

[The prepared statement of Ambassador Lyman follows:]

PREPARED STATEMENT OF PRINCETON N. LYMAN

The views expressed in this testimony are those of the author and not the U.S. Institute of Peace, which does not take policy positions.

Chairman Corker, Ranking Member Cardin, and members of the Senate Foreign Relations Committee, thank you for holding this hearing. It is an honor to appear before you today to present my views on the current civil war in South Sudan and how it may be brought to a close. The views I express today are my own and not necessarily those of the U.S. Institute of Peace (USIP), which does not take policy positions.

Overview

The civil war in South Sudan is one of the great tragedies in the world today. It also is undermining the stability of one of the most sensitive regions in the world, the Horn of Africa. Indeed, it is for that reason that the United States has been strongly engaged over more than a decade to bring peace to what is now Sudan and South Sudan. That commitment was exemplified with President George W. Bush's appointment in 2004 of former Senator John Danforth as Special Envoy for Sudan, to help bring about the Comprehensive Peace Agreement (CPA) that ended the war between the north and south of Sudan that had gone on for more than seventeen years. The U.S. commitment continued under President Obama with similar senior level appointments and with constant and close U.S. attention to implementing the CPA, the culmination of which was South Sudan's gaining, peacefully, its independence in 2011.

U.S. engagement is no less critical now as it has been in the past in addressing this new crisis. I can imagine the feeling of despair and indeed anger in the U.S., especially among the long-time supporters of the Sudan peace process, that the leaders of South Sudan have so betrayed their people and wasted the opportunity that independence provided. That makes it harder to gear up for even more effort by the U.S. But the needs of the South Sudanese people are great with nearly 2 million people displaced and more than 7 million in desperate need of food aid. The U.S. already has spent more than $1 billion on humanitarian assistance in this situation. The threats to regional stability are also no less great than in the past when this area was engulfed in war. We are, finally, invested in this process. Walking back would be morally wrong.

The African lead

But our role as in the past is integrally linked to what the Africans do. It was the neighboring African countries who led the negotiations of the CPA and enabled us to play our role in support. It was the Africa Union's High Level Implementation Panel, led by former South African President Thabo Mbeki, which led the hard but ultimately successful negotiations implementing the CPA, to which again the U.S. could thus lend strong support.

Today the neighboring African countries under the Intergovernmental Authority on Development (IGAD) lead the peace process in South Sudan backed by the Africa Union and other AU members. African leadership is an essential element in bringing about peace. For it is the African countries, especially the neighbors, who are most affected by the crisis and who are also in the best position to enforce whatever international pressures are placed on the parties. Moreover, it is clear from past experience that if the African countries in a crisis situation are divided, the U.N. Security Council will be similarly divided on the steps to be taken, or even if united be unable to enforce any strong sanctions on the parties.

Unfortunately, IGAD is divided over this current crisis, making it difficult for it to take strong action. Though it frequently threatened an arms embargo and other sanctions on the contenting parties it never reached consensus on them and never recommended such to the U.N. Security Council. Members Uganda and Sudan are sharply divided politically and for a time have used the situation to carry out a proxy war between them. Ethiopia and Kenya have differed at times over how to move the peace process forward. Several of the members, and/or their private sectors, are involved in the arms trade or other economic activities that militated against supporting economic sanctions or an arms embargo. Somewhat to address these problems, the AU created IGAD Plus Five, adding other African countries to the process, which has helped in some ways to get more traction but added new and sometimes competing processes to the mix. Finally IGAD Plus was created which opens the door to broader international participation, including the U.S., UK, Norway, China, the Arab League, and others.

Despite its problems, IGAD has achieved much. It began with an impressively comprehensive approach to what would be required to bring lasting peace to South Sudan. It envisioned a broadly based process of political transformation covering reform of most of the political, social, and economic institutions of the country. Little by little, however, as the contending parties proved unresponsive to every effort to stop the fighting, breaking every cease fire agreement and proving impervious to threats of sanctions and punishment, IGAD moved to what might be described as a lowest common denominator for a peace process. That is, the two contenders—Salva Kiir and Riek Machar—would be called upon to come together once more in a government of national unity and work out together the changes necessary. IGAD has put together, painstakingly, this peace agreement which both sides have now signed.

It is still on paper a most comprehensive agreement. It includes the fundamental transformational changes necessary for a lasting peace. But it is extremely fragile. It depends too heavily on the cooperation and commitment of the contending parties, especially the leaders Kiir and Machar to implement these far reaching reforms, but who in fact have little incentive to do so. It sets out transformational processes and procedures which are commendable but which cannot possibly be accomplished in the time frames proposed. Most important, these reforms are unlikely to be implemented without strong international involvement. It is thus so fragile as to be doubtful of success. But it is the only peace process under way. Doing everything possible to make it work is thus the best thing we can now do.

Fundamental weaknesses that threaten the agreement

As you know I served as the U.S. Special Envoy for Sudan and South Sudan from March 2011 to March 2013. I have spent many hours and sleepless nights seeking to understand what went wrong in South Sudan, and why the hopes and dreams of the South Sudanese people have been so tragically betrayed. But I do not want to provide a history here today nor attempt a full examination of what went wrong. That will be important over time, especially for our understanding of peace processes in the future. I do however want to point to those causes of the conflict that bear on the potential for resolving it, and in particular on the peace agreement which the parties have recently signed.

I commend to the attention of all those concerned with this crisis the report of the Africa Union's Commission of Inquiry on South Sudan, headed by former Nigerian President Olusegun Obasanjo. That report is hard to read because it lays out in horrific detail the human rights violations—committed by both side—in this conflict. But the report is more than that. The authors undertook a careful and extensive examination of the institutions that should have been bulwarks against the outbreak of civil war—the ruling party (SPLM), the legislature, the judiciary, the military, the police, and civil society. All of them were inadequate to the challenge of keeping the rivalries among the leaders from spinning out of control. Of those I want to emphasize two: the ruling party and the military. Without understanding the weaknesses of those institutions, the peace agreement as now configured will almost surely fail.

The SPLM

The Sudan People's Liberation Movement (SPLM) emerged during the second of South Sudan's revolt against the north as the dominant party in the south. But South Sudan did not win its independence largely through a political process as much as a military one. Throughout the civil war, the dominant institution in the revolt was the Southern People's Liberation Army (SPLA) and the various factions and militia that eventually unified under it. All the leaders of the SPLM have been drawn from the military. That remained true after independence. In sum, the independence movement in South Sudan, embodied in the SPLM, was a military one with a weak political wing. By contrast in South Africa the anti-apartheid movement was largely a political one, fueled indeed by civic action and civil violence, but the ANC—the leading party—was inherently a political institution with only a small military wing. The African National Congress (ANC) has thus been able to manage its political rivalries—every much as challenging—within the structures of the party and without national upheaval.

The SPLM does have important symbolic and national importance in South Sudan. But its weakness as a political institution was revealed when Vice President Riek Machar indicated his intentional in 2012 to challenge President Salva Kiir first for leadership of the party and subsequently for the presidency. Given the history of Machar in the 1990s and the reported slaughter of Dinka when he was leading a revolt against the SPLA at that time, this was a fundamental challenge, reviving ethnic rivalries and bitter memories. It was a crisis that would try the capabilities of a sophisticated political party. But in the case of the SPLM, the party mechanisms were far too easily set aside by the President. Bypassing the party machinery, suspending its Secretary-General, and taking an aggressive military response to the challenge, Kiir made the party largely irrelevant.

I raise this because there is some hope, pressed largely by South Africa and Tanzania that the SPLM could serve as the unifying institution in South Sudan, overcoming the fissures that developed between President Kiir and Vice President Machar. This was the basis of the so-called Arusha process, which operated parallel to that of IGAD and developed a set of principles that would allow for a new reunified SPLM government as a vehicle for peace and for reform. But the SPLM as a political institution does not have either the political support among the contending forces in South Sudan nor real dedication to common principles, especially to the principles of party democracy, for such a process to succeed. As has quickly become evident, the government of President Kiir has not honored the principles agreed in the Arusha process and the former Secretary-General of the SPLM—Pagan Amun—who championed the Arusha approach, is once again in exile. The SPLM may have an important role in the future political dispensation in South Sudan, but it is not able at this time to be the principal political vehicle for either peace or reconciliation.

The SPLA

The Sudan People's Liberation Army (SPLA) is the other institution that might have been expected to provide a sense of national unity and stepped in to prevent the breakdown that occurred. But throughout the Sudan-South Sudan civil war, there was in fact little unity among the South Sudanese fighting units. Abetted in many cases by Khartoum, various militias, usually ethnically based, broke with the main SPLA/SPLM and fought against it. In the run-up to the referendum on South Sudan's right of self-determination, Salva Kiir did a remarkable job of bringing all these various units together in support of independence and as part of a single national army. But it was an incomplete unity. The various entities were enticed in by generous payments and high ranks for the leaders, and little integration of forces. As pointed in the Commission for Inquiry, the SPLA had as many as 700 generals. Units with few exceptions remained ethnically based. Loyalty to the national army was fragile, with some militia going in and out of the system, requiring new negotiations, new payments, and new tentative agreements.

As the tension between President Kiir and Vice President Machar grew in 2012, President Kiir began creating a special Presidential Guard made up of people from his home area, and outside regular army control. This only exacerbated the divisions within the SPLA. In the aftermath of the events of December 2013, the SPLA fractured along ethnic lines with Neur and Murle based units decamping to the opposition under Riek Machar.

The point here is that the SPLA, either in its present form or recreated into the "unified" form as before the current civil war, cannot act as unifying institution. Security sector reform, creating a truly national army loyal to the state not to a single party or leader, is of course desirable, and is included in the plans of the peace agreement. But such reform will be extremely difficult to undertake given the composition of current units, the attitudes of today's leaders, and the lack of a unifying national political narrative or institution. That means that security for the peace process must come largely from outside.

Implications for the peace agreement

There are three conclusions from this analysis.

♦ One is that African countries and institutions—IGAD, the IGAD Plus Five, the AU Peace and Security Commission, the AU Commission—have to be united and firm in enforcing this agreement on the parties.

♦ Second, additional security must be provided to protect the proposed government of national unity and the reform process, as well as civilians caught up in the war.

♦ Third, only the international community can assure that the transformational aspects of the agreement—constitutional change, free elections, justice, protection of human rights and free speech, active civil society participation, reconciliation, economic and financial transparency and accountability, and security sector reform—will be acted upon. Neither of the leading contenders—Salva Kiir nor Riek Machar—have a stake in these processes. Indeed they will find them threatening to their continued and rivalling ambitions for the presidency of the country.

Thus there is a need for stronger action from Africa, the UN, and the U.S.

Africa's role

The peace agreement will only succeed if the AU and its members are prepared to enforce it. The agreement provides for a high level Joint Monitoring and Evaluation Committee, headed by former Botswana President Festus Moghae. To be effective in this role, Moghae should be accorded by the AU the authority of a High Commissioner, someone who can call the parties to order, demand performance, veto bad appointments, make his own appointments when there is inaction, and recommend as necessary sanctions or other pressures upon the parties. He must especially have authority over the financial and budgetary processes of the transitional government, for corruption and financial irregularity rank as among the most destabilizing and dishonorable aspects of the government including when Kiir and Machar were tougher in office. This is a tall order for the AU, but it is essential.

Second, the AU must select urgently the Judge of the Hybrid Court that is to address issues of justice arising out of the Commission of inquiry and its conclusions that crimes against humanity have been committed. Working hand in hand, President Moghae and the Hybrid Court can wield the necessary influence to force transformational change upon the parties.

Third, the AU must strengthen quickly the Ceasefire Transitional Security Arrangements Monitoring Mechanism (CTSAMM) which is to monitor the cease fire, cantonment of troops, and related matters. The CTSAMM moreover must add women to its ranks to assure that gender issues are being addressed in a context where much gender violence has and continues to take place. Its reports, which are to be made public, should provide the basis for firm action by IGAD, the AU and as appropriate the UNSC. Fourth the AU must conclude that security in Juba, a sine qua non for establishing the government of national unity, requires more than the security forces of the parties and creation of joint police units, as now envisioned in the security agreement. These security institutions are part of the problem and are very unlikely to work in concert or objectively. Right now not only has the opposition leader not come to Juba, but the arrangements for his doing so, with his own security contingent, is almost a predictor of violence. An enhancement of the U.N. Mission to South Sudan (UNMISS), or a related AU force is necessary.

The U.N. role

UNMISS has done an extraordinary job in the midst of this conflict. Some 200,000 civilians have been taken into UNMISS camps for protection and defended against attacks by belligerents. In spite of harassment and being shot at by forces from both sides in the conflict, UNMISS continues to send out patrols, facilitate humanitarian aid, and as much as possible protect the 1.7 million displaced. It is shocking that the Government of South Sudan continues as it has for several years to speak out against UNMISS, have its forces fire on U.N. peacekeepers, and to denigrate its work.

The UNSC is scheduled to renew UNMISS's mandate this month. In doing so, it should expand the mandate to allow UNMISS to play a more active role in the securitization of Juba, and reinforce its protection mandate. Further, the UNSC should put the leaders of the SPLM and the SPLM/IO on notice in the strongest possible terms that any attack on U.N. peacekeepers is a war crime and will be investigated and adjudicated. The same should apply to attacks on aid workers, 41 of whom have been killed since December 2013.

The U.S. role

The U.S. will have to continue to play a major role in alleviating the humanitarian crisis caused by the war. Without that, there is little hope for the people of this war-torn country. The dedicated work of the U.S. Special Envoy, Ambassador Donald Booth, and his team has contributed greatly to the progress that has been made toward a peace agreement and their work must continue as well with strong support from the White House. But there is more that must be done to bring about an end to the war.

How can the U.S. be most effective? We have a good example from President Obama's actions during his visit to the AU in Addis in August. Obama took the opportunity to call together the leaders of IGAD and the contending parties and urge them to find agreement on a peace plan. He made it clear that the U.S. was prepared to add sanctions of its own on the leaders of the war, and to press for such from the UNSC if agreement was not reached. The meeting created more urgency and purpose within IGAD and helped bring about the peace agreement recently signed. As progress on implementing the peace agreement drags on—the lack of adequate security in Juba, the failure yet to create a government of national unity, the delay in appointments for the Hybrid Court, etc.—there is again need for high level U.S. pressure. At the next meeting of the IGAD Plus, Vice President Joseph Biden, should attend, He should inject the same level of urgency, readiness for U.S. actions, and support, that President Obama provided in Addis.

Second, the U.S. should be prepared to provide support to exactly those transformational elements of the peace agreement that are most in danger of being ignored. Many civilians who have been pushed aside by the war, and many more displaced from their homes, would be ready and willing to contribute to this process. The World Bank pointed out some years ago that more than half of peace agreements fail with the parties going back to war. One element in success is the participation of broad elements of society, not just the "guys with the guns." The Institute of Inclusive Security points out that the percentage of peace agreements that succeed rises dramatically to the extent that women are involved. Yet including civil society and meaningful women's participation in the peace process is always difficult. It is resisted by the belligerents, is often inhibited by lack of organization and skill by civil society, and is often set aside by mediators fixed upon getting the contending parties—the "guys with the guns"—to the table. The U.S. should provide financial and political support for civil society, women's groups and individuals, for the professionals assigned to constitution drafting committees and judicial reform, and for economic reform institutions, reconciliation processes, and other aspects of participation of non-belligerents in the transformation process.

Finally, the U.S. should defend strongly a free media—something the Government of South Sudan has drastically curtailed over the past three years. Since as early as 2012, journalist in South Sudan have been harassed, beaten and in some cases assassinated. As one recent example, the Free Voice, a peace programming group partnered with the U.S. Institute of Peace, was shut down despite it having no partisan leanings. A leading newspaper was shut down at the same time. These practices must be stopped and the perpetrators punished. With limited other outlets for expression of opinion and accountability, a free media is an essential adjunct to this peace agreement.

And if it fails

Given all its problems and fragility, this peace agreement may collapse. Even now fighting and atrocities continue. If it fails then the issue must be raised to an even higher level.

The issue must become the subject of a heads of state level meeting at the UN, with the strong participation of the U.S., along with major African heads of State, AU leaders, our European partners and major humanitarian organizations. There should be an agreement at that meeting on a series of steps to restrict the fighting, such as an arms embargo, a trade embargo (excepting food and medicine), a ban on access to financial institutions by the contending parties, if possible with China's and Sudan' support placing further oil proceeds for the government in an escrow account, and the beginning of investigation and adjudication of war crimes by the proposed Hybrid Court. Neighboring African states would have to agree to enforce the arms and trade bans and refrain from any armed or financial support to either of the parties. A joint UN/AU mediation would then be charged with reinstituting a stronger peace plan.

This is a tall order. It would require considerable high level and intensive diplomacy. But only by this level and degree of international unity could this war be brought under control should the current peace plan fail.

Thank you, Senators. I am happy to answer your questions.

STATEMENT OF JOHN PRENDERGAST, ENOUGH PROJECT, FOUNDING DIRECTOR, WASHINGTON, DC

Mr. PRENDERGAST. Mr. Chairman, Senator Cardin, Senator Kaine, thank you guys for your leadership. I am honored to be here with my two friends, and I want to associate myself with much of what they said.

This war has been hell for the people of South Sudan, but here is a twist that we do not often hear about. It has also been very lucrative for the leaders who have plunged this country back into war. "War crimes pay" has been the message. Therein lies the crux of the problem, I believe, with U.S. and broader international efforts to support peace in South Sudan and other war-torn states in Africa. We are not frontally addressing the violent kleptocracies that are at the core of wars and extreme violence in South Sudan, Sudan, Congo, the Central African Republic, Somalia, Burundi, the list goes on.

South Sudan and other countries that are listed above are not simply failed states as they are commonly referred to. They are actually hijacked states.

In South Sudan, competing factions of the ruling party, who have been competing for decades so it is no surprise, they have used state institutions and deadly force to finance and fortify networks that are aimed primarily at self-enrichment and brutal repression of dissent.

South Sudan leaders never seriously invested in building credible state institutions, despite the hundreds of millions of dollars that you were asking about earlier that the United States invested in that state-building exercise, because they wanted to ensure the absence of accountability. As Sarah Chayes has observed in other settings, probably in this chair—Afghanistan is most prominently where her work is best known—corruption is not an anomaly; it is the foundation of the intended system.

The missing ingredient, I believe, and this is a critical point for the Senate Foreign Relations Committee, the missing agreement ingredient in U.S. policy toward South Sudan and many of these other war-torn states that we worry about is financial and economic leverage.

The surest route to building leverage for the United States to have a bigger influence on peace and human rights in these African countries is by hitting the leaders of rival kleptocratic factions where it hurts the most—in their wallets. A hard target transnational search is required for the assets that have been stolen from South Sudan, from the people of South Sudan by their leaders over the past decade, with the aim of freezing and seizing and then returning the proceeds of corruption to the South Sudanese people, and by creating real consequences for those who have robbed the country blind and plunged it back to war.

You want to get the attention of the leaders pursuing power in South Sudan, go after their stolen assets. That, Mr. Chairman, is where I believe the Senate Foreign Relations Committee can make the biggest difference.

So I would like now to turn with my little time to five specific financial and legal mechanisms that the U.S. can pursue now to counter these violent kleptocracies fueling and profiting from wars like that in South Sudan. These authorities have been strengthened in the aftermath of 9/11 globally, but they are rarely used for human rights and peace. They are rarely used for the second-tier conflicts that most people give lip service to and then focus the tools on primary objectives like Russia, rightly, Ukraine, North Korea, and Iraq.

The first recommendation I make is, in order for targeted sanctions, which is our basic tool, to actually have an impact, they have to be much more robustly imposed and much more systematically enforced than what is occurring presently for South Sudan and any of the conflicts that I have listed. We should be sanctioning a much wider group of perpetrators and their enablers in the international systems—banks and other entities—and enforcing those sanctions wherever we can.

We do that by building and leading—and you guys have primarily focused on this point of leadership—leading a broad alliance of countries to join us in these kinds of efforts, because we know, and you talked to Ambassador Power yesterday, you know the Security Council faces an incredible logjam because of Russian and Angolan and other countries' intransigence in the use of tools of financial leverage.

So we need to lead it. We need to get the countries where all these assets are parked and work with them to go after this money.

The second recommendation I would put forward is for the full Senate in 2016 to pass the Global Magnitsky Human Rights Accountability Act, S. 284, which has been introduced by Ranking Member Cardin and a number of other members of the Senate Foreign Relations Committee to bolster the U.S. Government's infrastructure to take action against those who commit human rights abuses or are complicit in major acts of corruption. That would provide a powerful tool of leverage for the United States.

The third recommendation I would put forward is identifying and countering sanctions busters. That should be a critical component, going up the value chain where money is really made in the international system off the human misery in these African conflicts.

I have a lot more in the testimony. I would be glad to talk to further about that.

The fourth recommendation I put forward is that sanctions are just one lever that can be used to apply financial pressure and build leverage. We also need to use the anti-money-laundering measures of the U.S. Treasury Department's Financial Crimes Enforcement Network, FinCEN, which has broad authority over under Section 311 of the PATRIOT Act.

We can require domestic financial institutions and agencies to implement specific special measures against designated primary money laundering concerns like that going on in South Sudan. You would be shocked at how much money these leaders are making off of money laundering today in South Sudan. We would like to see FinCEN issue an advisory to all U.S. financial institutions regarding the risk of money laundering activity in South Sudan.

My fifth and final recommendation has to do with mechanisms beyond the Treasury Department that the U.S. can bring to bear right now on South Sudan. The U.S. Government can take steps to ensure that the South Sudan leaders' ill-gotten gains do not wind up in the United States or pass through the U.S. financial system. Remember, money transfers represent perhaps up to 60 percent, 70 percent of the movement of money and the world, so there is a great vulnerability there for the U.S. to act.

The U.S. Department of Justice's Kleptocracy Asset Recovery Initiative is empowered to identify and seize the proceeds of overseas corruption in cases that involve a U.S. nexus. It just has to be investigated, found, and then acted upon. The kleptocracy initiative I think should actively pursue cases involving the misappropriation of South Sudan assets, especially given Senator Cardin's point about how much we have invested in South Sudan since its independence.

South Sudanese officials who loot state coffers—and that includes the rebels who used to be part of the South Sudanese Government and the current Government—should be under no illusion that they can park their ill-gotten gains in the United States or use the U.S. financial system to execute their heists.

As a closing note, we in the nonprofit world are trying to do our part by recently launching an initiative we are calling The Sentry. We have hired financial forensic investigators to follow the money and prepare substantial dossiers for action by the Treasury Department and other governments with jurisdiction over some of these stolen assets.

We will do our best in 2016 to shine a spotlight on these kleptocratic networks that are profiting from human misery in South Sudan and other countries, and make them pay for their crimes.

Thank you very much.

[The prepared statement of Mr. Prendergast follows:]

PREPARED STATEMENT OF JOHN PRENDERGAST

Chairman Corker, Ranking Member Cardin, and members of the committee, I'm grateful for the opportunity to testify about South Sudan at such a critical fork in the road for the youngest nation in the world. Working with the executive branch and through your actions, the Senate Foreign Relations Committee has the opportunity to help this new country change course and make progress on implementing the hard-won peace agreement that was signed back in August. If these efforts fail, South Sudan will likely be plunged back into a full-scale civil war that surely would be—based on past experience—one of the world's deadliest.

This war has been hell for the people of South Sudan, but it has also been very lucrative for their leaders. "War crimes pay" has been the message. And therein lies the crux of the problem with U.S. and broader international efforts to support peace in South Sudan and other war torn states in Africa: we are not frontally addressing the violent kleptocracies that are at the core of wars and extreme violence in South Sudan, Sudan, Congo, the Central African Republic, Somalia, Burundi, etc.

South Sudan and the other countries listed above are not simply failed states, as they are commonly referred to. They are hijacked states. In South Sudan, competing factions of the ruling party have used state institutions and deadly force to finance and fortify networks aimed at self-enrichment and brutal repression of dissent. South Sudan's leaders never seriously invested in building credible state institutions because they wanted to ensure the absence of accountability. Rather than protecting their populations, these competing factions used elements of the military and police to protect the spoils of their corrupt networks and their exploitation of the countries' rich natural resources. Then the two factions turned on each other due to long-running financial and political rivalries in the zero sum game that is South Sudan's politics, and they mobilized communities along ethnic lines, with predictably horrific consequences.

As Sarah Chayes has observed in other settings, Afghanistan most prominently, corruption is not an anomaly; it is the foundation of the intended system.

The hijacking of the state by corrupt leaders willing to use mass violence and harsh repression to maintain or gain power is the deepest root cause of South Sudan's war, as it is in a number of other endemic conflicts in Africa. But the outlook is not hopeless. The African states that have begun to overcome this cycle are beginning to thrive, offering rays of hope for the future of those still caught in conflict. And because these violent kleplocracies internationalize the spoils of their theft and use of deadly force, there are vulnerabilities that the U.S. is in a unique position to address in support of peace and human rights.

Our conventional diplomacy has limited value and impact because it has not sought to alter the calculations of those fueling and profiting from war. Therefore, dismantling the financial networks that enable and benefit from mass atrocities and creating a cost for profiting from conflict will allow other essential tools—such as diplomacy, peacekeeping, state building assistance, and accountability efforts—a better chance of success.

We must focus on making war more costly than peace. The incentives for financially benefiting from violence need to be fundamentally altered through a comprehensive strategy of financial pressure that provides the necessary leverage to drive the parties to compromise. As long as war is profitable for certain leaders and their enablers, it will be that much harder to end.

The missing ingredient in U.S. policy toward South Sudan, and many other wartorn African states, is financial/economic leverage. Greed is driving the calculations of South Sudan's government and rebel leaders. Politics in South Sudan has become a winner take all game, so huge patronage and security networks financed by acute corruption can only be maintained by keeping other factions out of government. The national interest is sacrificed for more venal self-interests as a matter of policy. And given the lack of any accountability for such a system, it should not be surprising that it continues.

When there are no limits to the hijacking of state resources or consequences for the use of violence to maintain power, instability and civil war are never far off. It is in the arena of global financial investigations into the proceeds of corruption used to fund mass atrocities that the U.S. has the most potential leverage. The U.S. and other governments working genuinely for peace in South Sudan (and other wartorn African states) can only enhance their influence in supporting peace and human rights if a concerted effort is made to expand economic pressure. And the surest route to building this kind of leverage is by hitting the leaders of the rival kleptocratic factions where it hurts the most: their wallets. A hard target transnational search is required for the assets that have been stolen from South Sudan by its leaders over the last decade, aiming to freeze, seize, and return the proceeds of corruption to the South Sudanese people and create a real consequence for those that have robbed the country blind and plunged it back into war.

That, Mr. Chairman, is where the Senate Foreign Relations Committee can help the most, and where I believe your efforts should be focused: ensuring that the U.S. government and its allies deploy the under-utilized tools available to build financial leverage in support of peace and human rights in South Sudan, Sudan, Congo, and other violence-wracked states in Africa. U.S. financial leverage remains strong when it is built and utilized. That is where we can make a difference.

More specifically, to build real leverage, we must focus on three key elements:

♦ Creating consequences for those who undermine the agreement's implementation or the spoilers who loot state assets;

♦ Supporting the peace agreement and the institutions it has established in South Sudan, especially those dealing with financial transparency and accountability; and

♦ Enhancing the capacity of civil society to do the same, holding their own leaders to account and countering extremist discourse.

Later in my testimony I will outline several specific measures that the United States government should pursue now in order to build needed leverage, but first I want to focus the Committee on the key aspect of how South Sudan descended into this conflagration. A proper diagnosis will yield more effective policy prescriptions.

Violent kleptocracy in South Sudan: a hijacked state

South Sudan is what the Enough Project defines as a "violent kleptocracy." It is a system in which the country's wealth has been captured and controlled almost exclusively by a small group of powerful elites within the government and the patronage networks and private sector operators connected to them. Ruling elites in Juba have relied on state institutions, especially the state security apparatus, to enrich and protect themselves at the expense of the rest of South Sudan's population. And they use extreme violence to enforce the kleptocratic system at the core of South Sudan's tragedy.

Although there are many causes, we see a corrosive climate of corruption and elite competition for state resources at the heart of South Sudan's current crisis. The South Sudanese Minister of Justice himself recently acknowledged that the pattern of corruption in his ministry and elsewhere is so pervasive that "everyone is stealing." The word "corruption" is mentioned no less than 34 times in a recent report by the African Union Commission of Inquiry on the crisis in South Sudan. One quote from the report, in particular, illustrates the centrality of corruption in the current crisis:

> It was clear from the various consultations of the Commission that the absence of equitable resource allocation and consequent marginalization of the various groups in South Sudan was a simmering source of resentment and disappointment underlying the conflagration that ensued, albeit the implosion of the conflict was brought about by the political struggle by the two main players. The struggle for political power and control of natural resources revenue, corruption and nepotism appear to be the key factors underlining the break out of the crisis that ravaged the entire country.

In South Sudan, the link between corruption and conflict could hardly be more pronounced. This link has been facilitated by the predominance of weak and underdeveloped institutions that allow for minimal or non-existent checks and balances on the excesses of government officials. For example, the country's systems for revenue collection, public expenditure, and currency management provide a select few individuals with privileged access to state resources. Senior government officials have been able to capture and divert national revenues and manipulate the official and black market exchange rates to turn huge profits on the dollar for themselves at the public's expense.

To protect their ill-gotten wealth, government officials spent a large portion of the national budget on security at the expense of infrastructure development, health, and education. State assets that are not looted outright are often used to fund elaborate patronage networks and to retain outsized security forces and the militias that are narrowly focused on protecting the elite within the government, often along ethnic lines, thus reinforcing these divisions between communities. And those who wield power rarely hesitate to use violence and commit the most horrific of human rights abuses to counter anyone who challenges their supremacy or seeks to expose their ruse.

These corrosive political and economic dynamics sowed the seeds for South Sudan's descent into violence in December 2013.

The violent kleptocracy that has emerged in South Sudan is also the product of long-standing exploitative economic practices with their origins in the 1983-2005 civil war in Sudan. Many of the existing patronage networks in South Sudan have their origin during that war. Patronage-based systems, however, can also be deeply unstable. In the case of South Sudan, rival cliques within the system started competing for control over the spoils of state power, leading to an increase in violence and state repression, and eventual civil war.

This is exactly what happened in late 2013. A political dispute between President Salva Kiir and Vice President Riek Machar may have been the proximate cause of the current crisis, but elite competition between rival factions over access to state resources was the major underlying catalyst of the conflict.

As the Enough Project details in a report to be released next week, the financing of the conflict is representative of the patronage networks and kleptocratic system that prop up those in power and sustain continuous violence. The government has been able to fund the conflict primarily with oil money and currency speculation schemes that leverage the difference between the official and black market exchange rates. It has also received loans on future oil production, and from doing business with "war profiteers"—private sector investors interested in gaining access to South Sudan's natural resource wealth once the conflict has ended.

For its part, the opposition funds the war with the personal wealth of key individuals in its ranks, through diaspora remittances, and from high-risk investors. Several opposition delegations have toured the United States, Canada, and Australia seeking financial support from members of the South Sudanese diaspora. These sources of funding are vital to sustaining the opposition because they lack access to the state's financial resources and do not receive regular salaries.

In retrospect, South Sudan's slide into a state of violent kleptocracy, corruption, and conflict seems like a predictable path. But that doesn't mean nothing was done to prevent these dynamics from taking hold. The legal and institutional frameworks to manage the petroleum industry and combat corruption in South Sudan actually exceed international standards in some cases, but implementation and enforcement have been non-existent. The problem is that laws are ignored and institutions are disempowered or marginalized because they are not in the interest of those in power.

The bottom line is that competing South Sudanese factions of the ruling party have been willing to loot state assets and murder rivals and civilians alike because they believe there are no consequences. To change the equation, consequences must be created.

Ending impunity and creating consequences in South Sudan

Ultimately, ending South Sudan's crisis will require creating accountability for economic and atrocity crimes. This is where the United States is in a unique position to both support the implementation of the peace agreement and pursue global financial measures to curtail conflict financing in South Sudan. My fellow panelists discuss the importance of U.S. support for accountability for war crimes through support to the proposed Hybrid Court, which I strongly support. I'd like to focus on five financial and legal mechanisms that the United States can pursue to counter the kleptocracy at the core of the war and enhance economic accountability in South Sudan:

- ◆ Enhancing the types of criteria used by the U.S Treasury Department to impose sanctions;
- ◆ Passing the Global Magnitsky Act;
- ◆ Ensuring that sanctions are enforced by Treasury once imposed;
- ◆ Directing the Financial Crimes Enforcement Network (FinCEN) to gather information and address potential money laundering activities; and
- ◆ Building cases at the Department of Justice-led Kleptocracy Asset Recovery Initiative to investigate and prosecute cases involving the U.S. financial system.

For many of the initiatives laid out below, the U.S. can act unilaterally as well as in partnership with the UK, EU, and others that have similar concerns and well-developed financial, legal, and regulatory frameworks to target assets, firms, and individuals under their jurisdictions. The impact would be greatest if the U.S. builds a coalition of countries willing to work with us in these efforts, particularly countries where South Sudan's leaders have stored their assets or housed their families. Deadlocks in the U.N. Security Council should not be a reason to not pursue multilateral leverage-building actions.

First, in order for targeted sanctions to actually have an impact, they must be more robustly imposed and systematically enforced. Moving forward, the U.S Treasury Department's Office of Foreign Assets Control (OFAC) should focus its investigations on politically and financially exposed individuals who threaten the implementation of the peace agreement and overall peace and security in South Sudan. This will likely require OFAC to issue intelligence community collection requirements to gather information on possible targets and their networks in South Sudan, the region, and overseas.

Additionally within this category, there are two ways that the sanctions authorities on South Sudan could be improved significantly, and members of Congress should encourage the Obama administration to pursue these steps. Facilitating public corruption in South Sudan should be grounds for designation under sanctions. At least five U.S. sanctions regimes (those for Belarus, Burma, Syria, Venezuela, and Zimbabwe) have included language that explicitly allows Treasury to place sanctions on anyone who facilitates public corruption. Sanctions can also be used to address attempts to muzzle civil society and the press. Civil society actors and journalists must be able to carry out their essential tasks in supporting implementation of the peace agreement and serving as watchdogs for the public trust against abuses perpetrated by state actors. The Executive Order recently issued on Burundi and the existing sanctions regime on Venezuela serve as a blueprint for countering public corruption and enshrining protections for civil society actors and journalists.

Second, in addition to use of the existing designation criterion within the South Sudan Executive Order related to the commission of the grave human rights abuses outlined in the African Union Commission of Inquiry report, Congress should pass the Global Magnitsky Human Rights Accountability Act, S. 284, introduced in the Senate by Ranking Member Cardin, to bolster the U.S. government's infrastructure to take action against those who commit human rights abuses or are complicit in acts corruption.

Third, we also should not forget about "sanctions-busters" and international facilitators that enable corruption. There is no shortage of unscrupulous illicit entrepreneurs, or "war profiteers," willing to help isolated regimes circumvent sanctions and remain financially afloat. Therefore, identifying and countering these sanctions busters must be made a crucial component of enforcement efforts, regardless of the original authorities used to impose sanctions. Current sanctions authorities already allow the Treasury Department to place sanctions on anyone found "to have materially assisted, sponsored, or provided financial, material, logistical, or technological support for, or goods or services in support of any of the [prohibited] activities—or of any person whose property and interests in property are blocked."

This provision cannot be an idle threat. Enforcement resources at OFAC should also be directed at those named as Specially Designated Nationals to ensure that they are not able to continue conducting business in ways that should be impacted by sanctions, but in some cases may not be because of insufficient resources for enforcement at Treasury, or a lack of cooperation from South Sudan's neighbors. Congress should supplement Treasury's resources to ensure OFAC has the resources it needs to enforce sanctions and monitor those designated, given the many priorities the agency is balancing.

Fourth, sanctions are not the only lever that can be used to apply financial pressure. Anti-money laundering measures should also be part of the equation. The U.S. Treasury Department's Financial Crimes Enforcement Network (FinCEN) has broad authority under section 311 of the Patriot Act to require domestic financial institutions and agencies to implement specific "special measures" against a designated primary money laundering concern. We would like to see FinCEN issue an advisory to all U.S. financial institutions regarding the risk of possible money laundering activity in South Sudan.

FinCEN's issuing such an advisory would trigger U.S. banking and financial institutions to provide information about money laundering activity to the Treasury Department. FinCEN could, in turn, use this information to determine if specific banks, classes of transactions or specific accounts should be designated as primary money laundering concerns. These steps could place significant pressure on the networks relied upon by corrupt officials, opposition leaders, and their enablers. Should FinCEN identify a primary money laundering concern, its special measures under section 311 could require specific types of information collection and due diligence or even prohibit U.S. financial institutions from maintaining correspondent accounts connected to the primary money laundering concern.

Finally, there are also mechanisms beyond the Treasury Department that the U.S. can bring to bear in South Sudan. For example, the U.S. government can also take steps to ensure that South Sudanese leaders' ill-gotten gains do not wind up in the United States or pass through the U.S. financial system. The U.S. Department of Justice's Kleptocracy Asset Recovery Initiative is empowered to identify and seize the proceeds of overseas corruption in cases that involve a "U.S. nexus." When appropriate, the Justice Department's Kleptocracy Initiative should actively pursue cases involving the misappropriation of South Sudanese assets. South Sudanese officials who loot state coffers should be under no illusion that they can park their ill-gotten gains in the United States or use the U.S. financial system to execute their heist.

Supporting South Sudan's peace deal

The peace agreement signed in August has ushered in some hope that South Sudan can move beyond the violence that has plagued the country for the past two years. The agreement represents an important milestone in efforts to end the conflict, but as long as South Sudan's kleptocratic system remains intact, the peace agreement will remain imperiled.

To be sure, the peace agreement signed in August contains provisions that, in theory, take aim at corruption and bolster accountability. For example, it stipulates the creation or reconstitution of several important domestic institutions with an anticorruption mandate, including the Anti-Corruption Commission, the Fiscal, Financial Allocation and Monitoring Commission, and the National Audit Chamber. These organizations must be effectively empowered to fulfill their mandate, just as the Hybrid Court must be fully empowered to address human rights violations.

The peace agreement also mandates the creation of the Joint Monitoring and Evaluation Commission (JMEC), a body of a few dozen representatives from regional and international actors that is supposed to monitor the implementation of the agreement. Empowering this entity to expose corruption and the misappropriation of state assets is a crucial priority for ending the culture of impunity among South Sudan's leaders. Donors must provide JMEC with the necessary resources and technical expertise to fulfill its mandate. These experts must include specialists in forensic financial accounting and oil industry transparency.

To enhance effectiveness, donors should also provide increased support to South Sudanese civil society to hold their leaders to account. Supporting the internal demands for peace, transparency, and human rights is an essential bottom-up element of a comprehensive strategy for sustainable change.

Moving forward in South Sudan, we need to beware of cosmetic reform. Fully supporting sustainable peace will require integrating anti-corruption and accountability initiatives into virtually every aspect of our engagement in South Sudan—and leaning on our partners to do the same. In other words, accountability and anti-corruption initiatives must be woven into everything from security sector reform to foreign assistance. It also means not necessarily accepting anti-corruption initiatives at face value. South Sudanese officials shouldn't be able to reap the rewards of compliance by simply paying lip service to reforms but rather should ensure that there is clear reporting on what actions are taken and what remains before further steps in assistance programs are taken.

Conclusion

Mr. Chairman, the Senate Foreign Relations Committee can make a difference in fighting kleptocracy in South Sudan by ensuring sufficient resources for agencies like OFAC and FinCEN and then holding them accountable for results on South Sudan, by passing legislation like the Global Magnitsky Human Rights Accountability Act, by strengthening language on sanctions to target the looting of state coffers and the repression of civil society, and by ensuring adequate resources so that the peace agreement can be enforced.

South Sudan has devolved into a violent kleptocracy in which we have seen atrocity after atrocity committed while the state's coffers are looted. We have a chance now to help South Sudan change course. The process of building effective, accountable institutions in South Sudan that are inherently different from what we have today will undoubtedly require significant resources, sustained engagement, and time. But unless economic and atrocity crimes at the root of the system are addressed, South Sudan will remain at risk of a return to deadly conflict. To prevent this, we urge you to ensure that the tools at the disposal of the U.S. government are deployed to the fullest extent in support of peace and accountability in South Sudan.

The CHAIRMAN. Thank you, sir.

Mr. Akwei?

STATEMENT OF ADOTEI AKWEI, MANAGING DIRECTOR, GOVERNMENT RELATIONS, AMNESTY INTERNATIONAL USA, WASHINGTON, D.C.

Mr. AKWEI. Thank you, Mr. Chairman and members of the committee, for the opportunity to present our analysis and our findings. We have prepared written testimony, which I hope will be entered into the record.

Mr. Chairman, members of the committee, it is hard to find words to do justice to the tragedy and the depth of suffering that the people of South Sudan are going through. When one adds on the human rights abuses that have impacted these people during the civil war in Sudan, which dates back to 1955 with a brief respite between the 1972 and 1983, the current conflagration and its primary drivers is even more appalling.

In all of that time, the international community has responded, and I would like to acknowledge the incredible leadership and resources that the United States has brought to the crisis. But often, we have done too little too late on various aspects of the conflict.

In the international community, we have consistently failed to uphold and impose accountability on the actors' link to abuses and the officials of the new government when they assume power after gaining independence. The people of South Sudan are reaping the grim consequences of that failure. These include war crimes of extrajudicial execution, mass killings, rape, the destruction of livelihoods, the destruction of homes, the humanitarian crisis, which has created over 2 million displaced persons, and of course the food insecurity that was referred to earlier in the first panel.

In addition to that, one of the more disturbing trends has been Sudan's initation of government repression and the closing of political space. Freedom of expression is heavily curtailed in South Sudan and the situation is worsening. Authorities, especially the National Security Services (NSS), routinely harass and intimidate human rights defenders and journalists. The NSS arbitrarily detains journalists and orders some to leave the country. NSS officers have shut down newspapers, seized copies of papers, and prohibited the publication of articles.

The weakness of the criminal justice system has resulted in rampant human rights abuses, such as pretrial detention, failure to guarantee due process and fair trials, and arbitrary arrests and detention.

State security forces are only contributing to the overwhelming culture of impunity and fear through their inability to hold perpetrators of human rights abuses accountable and arbitrary arrests and detention of journalists and human rights offenders. Further, the capacity of the police and the judiciary to enforce the laws has been decimated due to the militarization and defection of many police officers.

In addition to this, parliament, as you know, passed a national security bill. While President Kiir refused to sign it into law, the possibility of the bill becoming law remains and continues to be a threat and an act of intimidation. This bill would give the National Security Services broad powers to arrest, to detain without appropriate oversight mechanisms against such abuses, and continues to be a major impediment toward any kind of accountability, whether it be on the issues of corruption that John has referred to or more civil and political types of abuses.

Until persons linked to human rights violations are brought to justice, there will be no incentive to change behavior and no progress toward improving the respect and protection of human rights. We in the international community will be stuck in the same fire drill of trying to stop violence and in the process postpone setting up effective mechanisms of governance and accountability.

It is well past time for the United States, in concert with the A.U., IGAD, and the United Nations, to make abusive actions have consequences and begin to break the cycle of impunity in Sudan. The failure of leadership, which this hearing appropriately uses as its focus, that created the enabling conditions for the current crisis occurred in the country as well as outside of it. Until this is corrected, all of us share the blame of the continued suffering.

We have a number of recommendations, some of which have already been noted. We would continue to call for U.S. leadership in trying to push for a comprehensive arms embargo. We support an imposition of asset freezes and travel bans more robustly against individuals and entities who have engaged in violations of international humanitarian law and abuses of international human rights law.

We also feel that pressure must be put on the U.N. Security Council to act on the paper outlining options for accountability, for example, the hybrid court that you have referred to; the peace and justice and reconciliation initiatives; and, most importantly, the news that the United States is already beginning to collect evidence is probably one of the most important steps forward, because as soon as that evidence is lost, it becomes incredibly difficult to impose and enforce accountability later down the line.

Mr. Chairman, members of the committee, we really are facing, as John said, not just a failed state, but a hijacked state. It is a tragedy that it has happened so quickly. We must all redouble our efforts to try to change this.

Thank you.

[The prepared statement of Mr. Akwei follows:]

PREPARED STATEMENT OF ADOTEI AKWEI

Introduction

On behalf of Amnesty International USA we would like to thank the Members of the Senate Foreign Relations Committee for the opportunity to present our analysis and recommendations on the ongoing crisis in South Sudan.

Amnesty International's work in South Sudan

Amnesty International is the world's largest human rights organization, with more than 7 million supporters in over 150 nations and territories. There are 80 country chapters of Amnesty International. Here in the United States we have nearly 500,000 supporters whose dedication to human rights has impacted both policy and practice around the world.

Amnesty International has been seeking to protect and improve human rights in Sudan since its formation in 1961 and on South Sudan since it seceded from Sudan and gained its independence in 2011. AI has issued reports, held meetings with government representatives for South Sudan, and have also submitted reports to various U.N. and AU bodies.

Background to the conflict in South Sudan

Since the outbreak of conflict in mid-December 2013 between the government of South Sudan led by President Salva Kiir and opposition forces led by former Vice

President Riek Machar, neither side has showed any respect for international humanitarian law nor for the lives and human rights of civilians. All parties to the conflict attacked civilians on a massive scale, destroying and looting civilian property, raping and abducting women and girls, obstructing humanitarian assistance, and recruiting children into their armed forces. These acts contributed to tens of thousands of deaths, physical injuries, the displacement of over 2 million people, a total loss of livelihoods, destruction of property, and high levels of food insecurity and malnutrition. The U.N. High Commissioner reports that around 1.6 million people are internally displaced in the country, 200,000 of whom shelter in six UNMISS Protection of Civilian (PoC) sites and around 650,000 people have fled to neighbouring countries as refugees.[1] The rest are sheltering in swamps and forests, while others have been integrated by host communities in areas with little or no conflict.

Such abuses of international human rights and humanitarian law have had severe repercussions on the mental health of thousands of South Sudanese people. The outward signs of trauma and loss are accompanied by often invisible psychological wounds and scars of conflict.

Despite the signing of a peace agreement in August 2015 and subsequent ceasefire declarations by both sides, violence has continued in Unity and Upper Nile states. Alarmingly, the conflict has encroached into Western and Eastern Equatoria states with clashes between the Sudan People's Liberation Movement and armed groups leading to displacement, loss of lives and destruction of property and contributing to egregious human rights abuses, the displacement of millions of people, the destruction of property and livelihoods and widespread food insecurity.

The Peace Agreement set out a large number of commitments, including constitutional, governance and security sector reforms. The peace agreement also provides for three mechanisms related to transitional justice—a truth and reconciliation commission, a hybrid court and a compensation and reparations authority. Implementation of the peace agreement has been slow at best, with most milestones to date having been missed, and with armed conflict and violence in the country continuing and in some areas, such as Western Equatoria, growing worse. South Sudan. To our knowledge, no progress has yet been made on the transitional justice mechanisms.

The international response

Despite international and regional efforts to establish peace, conflict and human rights violations continue unabated. On December 24, 2013 the U.N. Security Council approved an increase of the United Mission in South Sudan (UNMISS) to 12,500 troops and increased the mission's police force to a maximum of 1,323 personnel. The UNMISS mandate was revised in May 2014 to focus on protecting civilians, monitoring and investigating human rights, creating conditions that facilitate the delivery of humanitarian assistance, and supporting the efforts to cease hostilities. The U.N. Security Council has met to discuss changes to the mandate of the 12,500-strong United Nations peacekeeping mission to support early steps in the peace accord such as ceasefire monitoring which included U.N. Secretary General Ban Ki-moon's request for 500 extra troops and 600 police, along with helicopters and drones to help the mission enforce the peace deal. (NMG)[2]

Key human rights concerns

On October 27 2015 the long delayed report of the African Union Commission of Inquiry (COI) on South Sudan became public and reiterated the appalling human rights violations and abuses perpetrated against the people of South Sudan . The report finds unequivocally that both sides to the conflict including Salva Kiir's Government forces and the Opposition forces led by Riek Machar—have committed war crimes. This report only covered the period of the conflict until mid-2014, and to our knowledge, there has been no continuing investigation or follow-up.

The AU COI report documents people being burnt in places of worship and hospitals, mass burials, women of all ages, elderly and young, being brutally gang raped, and left unconscious and bleeding. People were not "simply shot, they were in some instance subjected to beatings before being compelled to jump into fire". The Commission heard of reports of some captured people being forced to eat human flesh or forced to drink human blood.

---

[1] UNHCR Global Appeal 2015 Update. OCHA Humanitarian Bulletin, December 2015, http://reliefweb.int/sites/reliefweb.int/files/resources/OCHA—SouthSudan—humanitarian—bulletin—1Dec2015.pdf

[2] South Sudan Government Directs Civilians to Leave UN Base, The Citizen, December 4, 2015.

Human rights violations included extrajudicial killings (murder), sexual and gender based violence (SGBV), violations of freedom of expression and of the media, and discrimination entailed in targeting of individuals on grounds of ethnic origin.

Other crimes, which could constitute either war crimes or crimes against humanity are killings/murder, rape and sexual violence (SGBV), forced displacement/removal of populations, abducted children associated with conflict used in servitude and beaten, looting, pillage and destruction of property, enforced disappearances by state actors, torture, targeting of humanitarian workers and property.[3] The report tracks closely with concerns expressed by international human rights organizations, like Amnesty International as well as humanitarian organizations.

2015 has seen an intensification of these kinds of abuses rather than a decrease. The Office of the High Commission on Human Rights (OHCHR), UNMISS, Amnesty International and other organizations reported that between 29 April and 12 May this year at least 28 towns and villages in the Unity State have been attacked. These attacks by government forces on civilians and the resulting civilian displacement reflect the conflict driven human rights violations of early 2014. In Bentiu, the murder, abduction and sexual assaults on civilians not continue, but are escalating at an alarming rate.

On 30 June UNMISS issued a report with findings of widespread violations against civilians marked by a new brutality and intensity committed by government forces in southern parts of Bentiu. Moreover, UNICEF estimates that approximately 16,000 children have been recruited by all parties to serve in armed forces and groups.

Those who fled violence in Rubkona, Guit, Koch and Leer counties describe how government forces, mostly from the Bul section of the Nuer ethnic group, have been attacking their villages with axes, machetes and guns. Armed groups have also participated in the mass killing of civilians.

On 25 April, an armed group with machine guns, large guns, and RPGs attacked the Atar village in Piji County and shot anyone they saw. Those who survived these attacks sought refuge at U.N. protection of civilian sites. Intense fighting between the Sudan People's Liberation Movement/Army-In Opposition, government forces, allied youth and militia groups have caused thousands to flee to a United Nations base in Bentiu.

Government soldiers have targeted and killed people based on ethnicity and assumed political affiliation. Parties to the conflict have attacked hospitals and places of worship where civilians have taken refuge/sheltered. Currently the culture of impunity allows these abuses to go unchecked. Perpetrators need to be held accountable for their actions to deter further atrocities.

Deepening humanitarian crisis

South Sudan is in dire need of humanitarian assistance due to the conflict and as a result of civil war in Sudan that preceded the country becoming independent. In October, the U.N., FAO and WFP issued a report stating that "3.9 million people in South Sudan faced severe hunger and that tens of thousands were on the brink of famine." [4]

The obstruction of humanitarian assistance by parties to the conflict is also a significant roadblock to delivering lifesaving assistance. Parties to the conflict have attacked humanitarian workers and U.N. bases where an estimated 180,000 people have sought shelter. Five humanitarian workers have been killed, two U.N. employees abducted and three crew members killed when their UNMISS helicopter was shot down. The International Committee of the Red Cross announced the withdrawal of staff from Leer County in October and there are reports that other agencies have also been weighing whether their staff can stay and operations can be continued.[5]

Government repression

Freedom of expression is heavily curtailed in South Sudan and the environment for journalists, human right defenders and civil society to do their work without intimidation or fear has greatly declined.

On October 8, 2014 the Parliament passed a National Security Service Bill. However, President Kiir refused to sign it into law and sent it back for revisions. Despite this, the bill purportedly came into law in March 2015. The ¢Act gives the National

---

[3] Final Report of the Africa Union Commission of Inquiry on South Sudan, African Commission of Inquiry on South Sudan, Page 117, October 15, 2015

[4] http://www.wfp.org/news/news-release/un-calls-immediate-access-conflict-affected-areas-prevent-catastrophe-south-sudan

[5] https://www.icrc.org/en/document/south-sudan-conflict-leer-looting-icrc-forced-withdrawal.

Security Service (NSS) broad powers to arrest and detain without appropriate oversight mechanisms against abuse. Emboldened by this, the NSS have arrested, harassed and intimidated journalists, civil society actors and perceived political opponents. They have also held temporarily or confiscated entirely issues of multiple newspapers.

Moreover, a draft Non-Governmental Organizations Bill remains a possibility after being considered by Parliament. This bill would restrict the right to freedom of association by requiring registration, prohibiting NGOs from operating without being registered, and criminalizing voluntary activities that were carried out without a registration certificate.

Need for accountability

Even though the government of South Sudan did set up inquiries into conflict related abuses following the start of the conflict, none of these have resulted in independent and effective investigations or accountability.

After the start of the conflict, President Kiir formed a committee to investigate human rights abuses. The committee submitted a report to the President in December 2014; however, it has yet to be released to the public. Furthermore, the SPLA set up two investigation committees in December 2013. Approximately 100 individuals were arrested, all of whom escaped during a gunfight among soldiers in March 2014. While the SPLA has announced that it has rearrested two individuals, no information was made public about their identity or the charges against them.

On 2 July, the Human Rights Council adopted a robust resolution on South Sudan, which requested the OHCHR to undertake a mission to South Sudan and to recommend follow-up actions for the Human Rights Council, including the possibility of a mechanism, such as a Special Rapporteur. The appointment of a Special Rapporteur to South Sudan will be a critical affirmation by the international community toward their obligation to ensure accountability and justice for human rights abuses and violations of international humanitarian law.

Perhaps most urgently the international community must act swiftly to establish and implement accountability investigations now—without waiting for the full establishment of the hybrid court or the appointment of a Special Rapporteur. This is critical to help preserve evidence and for eventual prosecutions in the future.

Conclusions

Mr. Chairman, members of the Subcommittee, it is hard to find words to do justice to the tragedy and depth of suffering that the people of Sudan are going through. When one adds on the human rights abuses that have impacted the same people during the civil war in Sudan which dates back to 1955 with a brief respite between 1972 and 1983, the current conflagration and its primary drivers, is even more offensive. In all of this time the international community has often done too little too late on various aspects of the conflict but it has consistently failed to uphold and impose accountability and the people of South Sudan are reaping the grim consequences.

The title of these hearings is a stark reminder of how badly all of us, the leaders of South Sudan's government, and the armed groups, the leaders of the African Union and IGAD and the international community, have failed the people of South Sudan. While it might have been woefully optimistic to expect strong governance and the rule of law to immediately manifest itself in South Sudan after nearly 60 years of conflict no one appears to have anticipated the conflagration that is destroying the country now.

Until persons linked to human rights violations are brought to justice there will be no incentive to change behavior and no progress toward improving the respect and protection of human rights and we in the international community will be stuck in the same fire drill of trying to stop violence and I the process postpone setting up effective mechanisms of governance, accountability. It is well past time for the United States, in concert with the AU, IGAD and the U.N. to make abusive actions have consequences and begin to break the cycle of impunity in South Sudan.

AMNESTY INTERNATIONAL'S RECOMMENDATIONS

We urge you members of the Senate Africa subcommittee to:

Support the implementation of the human rights and humanitarian provisions in the Agreement on the Resolution of Conflict in South Sudan;

Take measures to ensure that all parties to the conflict cease violations of international humanitarian law and violations and abuses of international human rights law;

Call on the government of South Sudan to adequately protect internally displaced populations, ensure their security, and help create conditions that would allow them return or safely relocate in accordance with their wishes;

Support efforts to ensure access to justice and reparation programs for victims of human rights violations and abuses including on the establishment and operationalization of a hybrid court;

Call upon the U.N. Security Council to impose a comprehensive arms embargo against all parties in the conflict on South Sudan; and

Call upon U.N. Security Council to impose sanctions against individuals and entities who have engaged in violations of international humanitarian law and abuses of international human rights law.

The CHAIRMAN. Thank you, all. We appreciate the work that each of you do and the organizations that you represent.

Ambassador Lyman, just in hearing you talk about the fact that two leaders really are not committed to this peace agreement, and then, John, listening to you and hearing how profitable it is for the two leaders to be extorting and extracting resources from their own country, and then to know now, since the peace agreement has been reached, both the opposition and the country leadership itself is now here asking us for money to implement the peace agreement, which is pretty unique, I have to say that while we do not want to undermine the process and do not want to talk about plan B, it does seem to me that if the leaders are not committed to it, if they are profiting from the kleptocracy that exists there, how should we view what is occurring there?

I mean, I think the independence of South Sudan occurred because of us, mainly. Yet we have obviously very corrupt leadership on both sides. How do we expect this peace agreement to actually bear fruit?

Ambassador LYMAN. Senator, I think Ambassador Booth put it well, to say that for the moment we should try to make this agreement work, if at all possible.

When I said that neither President Kiir or former Vice President Machar are committed, they are certainly not committed in my view to the long-term transformations and reforms that are needed. They may be led by pressures by arms embargoes and other things to need to end the conflict. I think doing everything we can to improve those incentives in the ways that we have all been talking about is important.

I think empowering President Moghae much more and putting real power in his hands to push the parties forward will also help.

I think it would be a mistake to jettison this agreement and walk away from it when so much work has been put into it. We have to recognize where those weaknesses are and press forward.

If, with all of that, then it just simply does not work, you have to build up to what I suggested, a new and much higher level approach, but on paper, this agreement makes a lot of sense. But it relies too much on trusting those two to work together. I think much more pressure has to be brought to bear to make that even possible.

Mr. PRENDERGAST. A quick footnote to what Ambassador Lyman said. I think I would make one small adjustment. I am sure it is not really a disagreement at all. It is really that you can pursue both tracks at the same time. I think that is what panelists can do as nongovernmental actors and the Senate Foreign Relations

Committee can do so effectively, and you have so effectively so
many different times, and that is, while pressing and pushing and
pursuing the implementation of this existing agreement, which by
the way does provide an exit ramp off a one-way road to hell that
South Sudan is on. We have to stop the bleeding. This agreement
allows for that possibility, if fully implemented.

But at the same time, this is really only the sort of small nuance
from what Princeton said, at the same time, I think we should be
putting in place now some of these elements that you would con-
sider plan B. Part of them would be the kind of things that I was
talking about where there are real financial accountability mechanisms and then particularly accelerating and pressing and pushing
the legal accountability measures that both of my colleagues have
talked about.

So I think pushing both forward much more robustly at the most
senior level we possibly can and building a multinational coalition
of countries who can act when the Security Council cannot because
of the divisions within it.

The CHAIRMAN. I very much appreciated your testimony. I know
Senator Cardin did, too. You are, in essence, arguing that we begin
collecting the stolen resources that both the president and the opposition have engaged in. I assume you are also talking about beginning sanctions efforts.

I hear Ambassador Lyman talking about the fact that while they
are committed, they are committed for the short term. They are not
committed for the long haul. In other words, they would like to buy
some time but revert to the same activities that they have been involved in after the short term.

Is that what I am hearing you say?

Ambassador LYMAN. I just do not think that you could expect
them to be committed to a real new constitution, clean elections,
and accountability that might, as you suggested, leave them both
ineligible to be president at the next election.

The CHAIRMAN. It sounds to me, you never want to prejudge, but
based on the evidence that it would leave them both in jail and
without resources.

So again, I do not know. I hear everybody talking about this
agreement as the best agreement on paper. We are dealing with
people. People usually act in their own self-interests. By pursuing
the route you are talking about, which sounds interesting to me,
John, but hearing the backdrop that Princeton is laying out, it does
not sound to me that going in that direction is going to lead to
places.

It sounds to me like some of what we heard yesterday, Senator
Cardin, where, unless you are going to somehow or another absolve
these two leaders of their wrongdoings and let them continue to
have the resources that they have stolen from their own citizens
and probably from us, let us face it, that there is no way this peace
agreement is going to come to fruition.

So if you would, is that a fair statement or not?

Ambassador LYMAN. Well, I would put it this way. It is a very
fragile agreement for exactly those reasons. However, you have to
remember, there is more in South Sudan than these two leaders.

There are others who are deeply concerned about this kind of transformation.

One of the recommendations I made is that the U.S. invest heavily in enabling them to play a role, professionals who have been pushed aside, judges who can come into the system, women's groups, others who can add real substance to this peace process.

But second, it seems to me, and this is why I think that the appointment of the head of the hybrid court should be now, is that the head of the hybrid court and President Moghae working together can hopefully put pressure enough on those who are culpable that eventually they will step aside.

Now that is going to take a real effort on their part, and that is why I was distressed to hear the timing on the hybrid court is so late.

Parallel to that, and picking up on what John said about parallel actions, as I mentioned, there is a report that will go to the U.N. very specifically on who is blocking the peace and who is attacking peacekeepers. That gives the Security Council a role to play on accountability.

There is also information not yet public behind President Obasanjo's Commission of Inquiry that also names names. That part of the report has not been made public.

So there is a lot of evidence that, if I can put it bluntly, can be used as pressure on the parties to eventually have those who are the real perpetrators and the obstacles step aside for a real transformation process.

The CHAIRMAN. Yes, sir, go ahead.

Mr. PRENDERGAST. Thank you very much. I would just turn it upside down, the whole question.

I would argue that the lack of accountability for war crimes and for mass corruption ensures continued instability and conflict. You have to break the cycle at some point. It is very unpredictable what happens when you break that cycle.

The threat of serious consequences, in my view, the actual imposition of serious consequences is the one thing that can change calculations of parties that for decades have destroyed their country and seen simply no cost for that.

Political transitions from one leadership to the next leadership group, if they are resisting it, are inherently highly unstable and unpredictable. What we as the United States can do is introduce some of these consequences and costs for the commission of these war crimes and crimes against humanity and mass theft of resources of the country. We can introduce these consequences in order to affect calculations.

And maybe look at a country like Liberia, where you actually had an international effort, which worked assiduously for transition. Had Charles Taylor simply complied with the conditions of his asylum, he would be today enjoying a nice life in Nigeria. But he did not.

In other words, we do not know where these guys will end up. They do not all have to end up in The Hague. There are different ways to do it.

But unless you start the ball rolling where they start to see the game is up, their number is going to be called, they are not going to change, I do not think. We cannot manage it how it is going to happen, but we can start the process.

The CHAIRMAN. I do not think you will have any debate here on that approach. I just think, in taking that approach, which to me is the right approach, you are very unlikely to have the leader of the opposition and the leader of the government working toward the peace agreement that we are talking about right now.

So it is quite a conundrum. Personally, I see failure.

I will now turn to our ranking member.

Senator CARDIN. Well, Mr. Chairman, we should also point out that the peace agreement envisions that these two individuals are going to be president and vice president. I do not want to prejudge their culpability. I really do not. I mean that sincerely.

But it does point out that there needs to be a plan B. I think this panel has been very, very helpful in understanding what a plan B looks like.

I do not disagree that you can do two things at one time. You can pursue a peace agreement and you can pursue the alternatives. I think what you have suggested, particularly on accountability, is very much part of the future of South Sudan.

The embargoes, I very much understand that. We need to work with the African Union. That is absolutely essential in order to be able to enforce that. All of that is understandable.

We certainly want to maintain the humanitarian assistance to the people. But we also have to understand that unless you have an effective way to get that humanitarian assistance, you cannot rely upon government networks that could divert those sources to fund corruption. So you have to also be careful that you just do not do things because it sounds good. It has to effectively be able to get to the people who are in need. That is where I think you have been extremely helpful.

Obviously, corruption is a huge issue here.

Mr. Prendergast, your comments really struck home. We very much want to be able to prevent the corrupt officials from being able to enjoy the fruits of their corruption by parking them in U.S. banks or visiting their properties in the United States.

Where do they try to keep their resources? Do they keep it in South Sudan? Are they trying to move it around?

Mr. PRENDERGAST. Well, you hit the nail on the head. Very rarely do you see kleptocratic leaders keep their money under their mattresses in their home countries. They internationalize the profits almost immediately in the form of real estate and front companies and all kinds of different investments. Their families live fairly lavish lives, and this is all while their country is being immiserated.

So what we are doing now is, because the collection priorities right now for the United States Government are, understandably: Russia because of Ukraine, ISIS, Iran, and a number of other high-priority targets, we have decided to fill the gap in U.S. collection efforts, intelligence collection efforts, privately. We are building a team or expanding a team to put together the dossiers that the United States Government, the British Government, other governments that have a jurisdiction and authority, can then act on. We cannot subpoena records. But we can take the information trail right up to the bank account itself or the property records and all the rest of it.

So we are putting all those together. In the spring of 2016, we are going to launch fairly high profile publicly. But privately, we have been working very closely with various enforcement agencies in different governments around the world.

You often see these sanctions regimes will sanction a couple midlevel commanders who are fighting in the field. They do not have their assets anywhere else. They are not even people who are feeding off this kleptocratic network. So we have to go after a higher order of leader.

Senator CARDIN. I think that would be very helpful. Thank you.

Mr. Akwei, you have stated what I think all three of the witnesses on this panel have stated, and that is that until persons linked to human rights violations are brought to justice, there will be no incentive to change behavior, and no progress toward improving the respect and protection of human rights.

How do you see implementing a peace agreement under the terms that have been negotiated? How can that incorporate true accountability?

Mr. AKWEI. I think what Ambassador Lyman said is that you basically have to decrease the power and influence of the two main players that you correctly said it is not in their best interest to move this forward.

If you can bring in the kinds of civil society involvement to kind of diminish and to basically empower the people of South Sudan, then you begin to have an actual framework not only for building enduring mechanisms of accountability, but also for ensuring adherence to any agreement.

Absent that, you are left with two individuals who have a track record now of ignoring deadlines and obligations.

This is why the government's closure of political space is so dangerous. It is not just another inconvenient development. It is actually fundamentally blocking what is an essential plank of the peace agreement or any movement forward.

So the two have to go hand in hand. The accountability mechanisms the United States can push and show that these are going to be genuine, credible mechanisms that are going to hold people to account is one thing. But empowering and protecting and reinforcing the role of the actors that represent the people is probably just as important.

Senator CARDIN. Thank you.

Ambassador Lyman, your plan B, some of it we can implement ourselves by unilateral action by the United States. Some of this we can work with international organizations in order to deal with it. But a huge part of it depends upon the effectiveness of working with the African Union. What is the prognosis that the African Union has the will and can be effective?

Ambassador LYMAN. I agree with you completely, because they are right at the center of it. I think up till now, the African countries, partly because of different interests among them and for other historical reasons, have come up with what I would call the lowest common denominator peace agreement. It is good on paper, but it rests on a lot of things that we have talked about.

This is part of the high-level diplomacy that President Obama was doing in July and which I am urging the Vice President and others to do now, to work with the Africans and recognize this peace agreement is too fragile as it now works. Their interests are being undercut, if this war continues. Whatever individual interests might be there, the region will suffer greatly.

To bring them to doing things, which are very tough, in effect empowering that mechanism to become—in effect, putting South Sudan into receivership. The African Union does not like to do that to a sovereign government, but it has to move in that direction, or as we talked about in plan B, agreeing to very tough sanctions.

They have done this before. They did this years ago in Burundi when the surrounding countries enforced a trade ban and really brought the country around. They have to agree to an arms embargo that is enforceable. They have to agree to a trade ban. And I would add one other thing that is hard, because of the Chinese and the Sudan Government, eventually getting the oil proceeds into an escrow account, so you really deprive the contending parties of the resources to carry on the war.

Bringing the African countries to recognize that this process is too fragile now and take these additional steps, that is where the high-level diplomacy I think it needs to be.

Senator CARDIN. Thank you very much.

The CHAIRMAN. Senator Kaine?

Senator KAINE. Thank you, Mr. Chairman.

Thank you to the witnesses for your important work and your testimony.

One of the reasons I love this committee is I get a chance to educate myself on areas that I do not feel an expertise in. On this committee, I spent most of my time working on the Americas and on the Middle East. I lived in the Americas. I have done a lot of travel to the Middle East. But my time in Africa has been very limited. So I love coming to hearings like this so I can learn more.

Really, my questions are going to be, Ambassador Lyman, with respect to your last point, which is we can exercise a lot of power with respect to levers we have to try to enforce norms that we think are important. But if the norms are not the norms of the region, norms that the region thinks are important, and the region is not willing to enforce, then all the levers that we have I think will only have a modest impact.

If the region enforces the norms, we are dealing with this with ISIL right now, we are dealing with this in a lot of issues in the Middle East, and, frankly, we have dealt with this in the Americas too, people telling us, boy, we really do not like what Venezuela is doing, but they are not going to stand up and condemn. Or people telling us, hey, we really do not like what a particular government in the Middle East may be doing that is authoritarian, but we cannot stand up and publicly condemn it. It would be better if the United States did.

We see this everywhere, and yet what we have seen is our levers are dramatically reduced in effectiveness if the norm is not enforced by the region.

You talked about the need for high-level diplomacy with other African nations. One of the phrases you use is discussing to help them see that this war endangers them. I mean, do we really need to help nations that are right there see that the war endangers them? They see it. They must see it. If we see it from thousands of miles away, they see it.

But what are the obstacles, either to nations or a regional group of nations or the institutions in Africa, to standing up and saying, hey, this is unacceptable behavior?

You used the Burundi example. What would be some things that we could do to hasten a recognition, okay, we took these actions with respect to Burundi, we should take them with respect to South Sudan.

If it is us taking actions, I think the effect will be, frankly, de minimis. But if it is the region promoting a norm and we are helping underline and support a regional norm, we are going to have a lot more effect here.

So you might start, Ambassador Lyman, but if others have thoughts too, I would love to hear them.

Ambassador LYMAN. Thank you, Senator. You put it very well.

I think to unpack a little bit the limitations in the region, as well as the strengths, as I mentioned, earlier, some of those countries have different interests. At the beginning of this crisis, Uganda and Sudan saw themselves fighting for influence in South Sudan. Uganda sent troops in on behalf of President Kiir. Sudan probably sent some aid to Riek Machar.

That is gradually being unpacked. The Ugandans finally have pulled their troops out. That opens the door for lessening that. But it took a lot of diplomacy, a lot of effort by the Africans, by the Americans, et cetera.

The second thing is people are profiting from this. I mean, John has pointed out that people profit. People do profit. They sell arms. They do other things. They have economic interests. That has held things back.

Third, the region has not quite paid a big enough price. Yes, refugees flow in every direction, but it has not upset their stability to a great extent.

So on the other side there is a great deal of frustration in the region about the South Sudan crisis and the failure of the peace process so far.

So I think the opportunity, and if this agreement continues to be in trouble, is to build a recognition that much, much stronger steps need to be taken. The fact that they finally published President Obasanjo's Commission or Inquiry report—and I commend that report by the way. It is hard reading because of the terrible, terrible things that went on, but it is also a very good analysis of what the institutional weaknesses were in South Sudan. The fact that they finally published that said that they were not going to keep it secret.

That they selected someone as distinguished as President Moghae to step in and sort of be the overseer, a little movement.

But I think if things really fail, I think it is possible for all of them to get together and say we are going to have to do more. The costs are going to get greater for all of us, because the region—you have Somalia, you have problems elsewhere in the region—the region cannot afford over a long time this cancerous struggle.

And I think you can build that. And I think with the right politics and diplomacy, the Africans will come around to saying, yes, we agree. We have to ratchet it up because it is not working. It is just going to take a lot of effort.

Senator KAINE. Great.

Others? John, please.

Mr. PRENDERGAST. Building on what Princeton said, this is where economic strategy can support U.S. political diplomacy. Many of the ill-gotten gains, the assets are parked in neighboring countries. Many of the families are living in neighboring countries.

So, for example, just one example, the U.S. anti-money-laundering provisions that I talked about earlier, if enacted, would send a powerful signal to the banks in the region. That would get the attention at the senior most levels of those regional governments.

Second example, and Princeton alluded to it, the top trade partner for Uganda in the world is South Sudan. If you start affecting that relationship, which the war has already done, which is part of their calculation as to why they want to try to clean it, but if you accelerate the impact like with some of the provisions Princeton is talking about in his plan B, you will get their attention very quickly. And I think they would become much more robust supporters going forward of the stronger policy toward the protagonists in the South Sudan war.

Senator KAINE. Please, Mr. Akwei.

Mr. AKWEI. One of the narratives that we have to help build are these other voices. In other words, not just the big men deciding what is in their best interests, and then assuming that their best interests equates to their country's interest.

This is why political space and civil society in Sudan, it is linked to civil society and political space in the region and the continent. If you do not have that as a focus and have the U.S. continue to press for that and protect that space, you are not going to be able to have that kind of narrative that you are talking about being accepted as important enough to trigger political change.

I think that is obviously a much larger and longer challenge but it is critical in this case because just having the leaders of Uganda and Sudan decide and basically direct or dictate and impact activities and developments and progress is a recipe for disaster.

Senator KAINE. I really agree with you with respect to the civil society component of this. If you look at the Arab Spring, the nation that has probably done the best, though it is very fragile and they are under attack and their success invites attack because there are those who just do not want them to succeed, has been Tunisia.

Tunisia was notable for a very vigorous civil society, labor unions, physician organizations, bar associations. Probably a little bit because of the French model, they had a big civil society that was not government, that was not religious organizations, but kind of at critical times would act to keep things from going off the rails.

So the work that we do to create that civil space is an important part of the diplomatic mission.

I appreciate your testimony.

Thank you, Mr. Chair.

The CHAIRMAN. Thank you for being here. And thanks for your strenuous efforts here in the committee and for being such a responsible member.

We thank all three of you for being here. You all have so much wisdom and knowledge that is helpful to us not only on this subject, but others.

My sense is there will be action taken as a result of this particular hearing. So, again, thank you very much. We look forward to continuing our discussions.

If you would, we are going to leave the record open until Monday afternoon. You are likely to get questions from other members. If you would respond, we would greatly appreciate it.

The CHAIRMAN. Again, thank you for your service.

With that, the meeting is adjourned.

[Whereupon, at 11:37 a.m., the hearing was adjourned.]

ADDITIONAL MATERIAL SUBMITTED FOR THE RECORD

RESPONSES TO QUESTIONS FOR THE RECORD SUBMITTED TO
AMBASSADOR DONALD BOOTH BY SENATOR CARDIN

Question. The Peace Agreement calls for Security Sector Reform and for Demobilization, Disarmament and Reintegration (DDR).

♦ Please provide a detailed summary of the administration's plans related to support security sector reform including activities, funding and any conditions we are asking the South Sudanese to meet prior to beginning support for such reforms.

♦ Too many times after conflict DDR is not fully implemented. How can we ensure that DDR is fully implemented in the wake of the peace agreement? What specific lessons can be applied from past DDR processes in South Sudan?

Answer. Although we have had some discussions around security sector reform (SSR) and disarmament, demobilization, and reintegration (DDR) of former combatants, at this time it is too early to say what the Administration's support, including any funding, will look like. We believe that SSR and DDR will be critical elements of successful implementation of the peace agreement, and to that end the Special Envoy's office has organized and conducted two conferences to convene SSR and DDR experts for a discussion of lessons learned from past SSR and DDR efforts in South Sudan and elsewhere in Africa. We are also funding a military planning expert to assist the South Sudanese in conducting a Strategic Defense and Security Review as called for in the August peace agreement.

The central lesson from past DDR processes, as discussed at the conferences, is that the political will of all national leaders from opposing sides is necessary for any DDR process to be successful. Therefore, engaging the commitment of South Sudan's leaders will be a critical first step in determining whether and, if so, what types of DDR program(s) to support. As with reconstruction, we will need to see a commitment of South Sudanese resources to SSR and DDR along with engagement by other international partners.

Question. The report of the African Union Commission of Inquiry of South Sudan states that there are reasonable grounds to believe that the abuses amount to war crimes and crimes against humanity.

♦ Has there been any attempt by the government to arrest or detain those implicated in the report?

♦ Has the leadership of the SPLM-iO turned over anyone accused in the report for detention or otherwise attempted to hold perpetrators of such violence responsible for their actions?

Answer. The answer to both questions is no. The African Union (AU) Commission of Inquiry has not made public an annex from the report that names individuals the Commission has identified as responsible for crimes indicated in the report. We have been told that the AU Commission will turn over the annex to the Hybrid Court for South Sudan once it is established. We have concerns about fair trial protections in the absence of a hybrid court and the development of a system for the indictment, arrest, and trial of any accused perpetrators.

Question. The report of the African Union Commission of Inquiry of South Sudan indicates that lack of follow through on accountability in the Comprehensive Peace Agreement was a factor in the outbreak of recent hostilities. The African Union—in accordance with Chapter 5 of the peace agreement—has agreed to lead the establishment and operationalization of a Hybrid Court to hold perpetrators of serious violence accountable. Secretary Kerry announced $5 million to support accountability in South Sudan.

♦ How does the State Department plan to allocate the $5 million that Secretary Kerry pledged earlier this year for an accountability mechanism?
♦ Does the Administration envision direct financial support for the hybrid court?
♦ You mentioned in your testimony that there are organizations currently on the ground documenting and collecting evidence that could be used in criminal proceedings. Who is responsible for maintaining the evidence and how will it be used?

Answer. In May, Secretary Kerry announced our intent to provide $5 million to support justice and accountability in South Sudan. We intend to support the Hybrid Court for South Sudan provided for in the August peace agreement, and we are also supporting human rights documentation efforts more broadly. Subject to the availability of funds, we intend to provide $3.5 million to support a credible, impartial, independent, and effective accountability mechanism, which could include direct financial support to the hybrid court if it meets those and other criteria. We are in dialogue with the African Union, which has responsibility, along with the Transitional Government of National Unity, for establishing the court as provided for in the August peace agreement.The other $1.5 million announced by Secretary Kerry is being used to fund a human rights documentation effort, run by the State Department's Bureau of Democracy, Human Rights, and Labor (DRL), that will build the capacity of local organizations to gather information on relevant violations and abuses. Currently there is no central database for information regarding evidence of atrocities, and a number of organizations such as UNMISS and the Commission of Inquiry each maintain its own records; we anticipate, however, that through our documentation program we will be able to support the creation of a central database to maintain documentation of atrocities. Once the program is underway, implementers will recommend an independent entity to be responsible for such a database.

Question. The State Department has documented violations by the government of South Sudan of democratic freedoms since 2012, including "corruption, harassment of nongovernmental organizations (NGOs) and attacks on their workers, illegal detentions, intimidation of journalists, and detention by security forces."

♦ We are heavily critical of governments, such as the one in Khartoum, that engage in these practices. What actions have we taken to press the government in Juba to improve respect for constitutional rights and fundamental freedoms of its citizens?

Answer. In both public and private messaging, this Administration has been critical of the Government of South Sudan regarding a number of its actions, including those that jeopardize the peace process as well as those that restrict enjoyment of human rights and fundamental freedoms. Among the most prominent critical messages were Secretary Kerry's statement on March 2, 2015, condemning the government's failure to abide by the Cessation of Hostilities, and the public statement by National Security Advisor Rice on July 9, 2015, the occasion of South Sudan's National Day, in which she criticized the government's failure to make peace. We have also made public statements from Washington and Embassy Juba concerning interference with humanitarian assistance.In private engagement, Ambassador Phee and other Embassy officials press government officials at all levels regarding a range of troubling actions, including President Kiir's threatening remarks regarding journalists, the closing of newspapers by the South Sudanese security services, unlawful detentions of civil society activists, and the NGO bill, in addition to urging the government to immediately fulfill commitments from its signed joint communique with the United Nations to combat the country's epidemic of sexual and gender-based violence. We have also engaged senior South Sudanese government officials on the NGO bill on multiple occasions. Ambassador Phee most recently discussed U.S. concerns about the hostile treatment of journalists with Michael Makuei, the Minister of Information and Broadcasting and Government Spokesman, on December 14.

Question. Corruption has plagued the government of South Sudan since its inception. In 2012, barely a year into independence, President Kiir accused 75 ministers and officials of having stolen $4 billion in state funds. It ranks 171 out of 175 on Transparency International's corruption perception index. One analysis published in July states that "the country's elites have built a kleptocratic regime that controls all sectors of the economy, and have squandered a historic chance for the development of a functional state." Chapter III of the Peace Agreement calls for legislation establishing an Economic and Financial Management Authority (EFMA) to ensure transparency and accountability and oversee public financial management.

- How much do we estimate has been stolen due to official corruption in South Sudan?
- Has there ever been any credible effort to investigate, charge or convict a government official of corrupt acts?
- What, if any, discussions have taken place relative to the development of the implementing legislation creating EFMA?
- Has the development of such legislation been a priority in our diplomatic discussions with the government of South Sudan?
- There are supposed to be donor representatives on the Authorities Board. Have we been approached to participate?

Answer. Numerous international independent watchdog organizations have alleged widespread official corruption in South Sudan and we have consistently reported in our annual Human Rights Report and elsewhere that corruption remains a pervasive and concerning issue. Anecdotal evidence supports these claims; however, thus far, there have been no reliable data that precisely capture the total cost of corruption or the amount of funds diverted as a result of official corruption. We are considering ways to improve our ability to detect and deter official corruption in South Sudan.

As outlined in Chapter IV of the Agreement of the Resolution of the Conflict in the Republic in South Sudan (ARCSS), the Transitional Government of National Unity (TGoNU) is required to establish the Economic and Financial Management Authority (EFMA) within four months of the transition. Although the TGoNU has not yet been established, creating the space for an active and effective EFMA is a U.S. priority, and we continue to engage both the Government of South Sudan and the opposition, in addition to the leadership of the Joint Monitoring and Evaluation Commission regarding the importance of immediately establishing and providing the necessary political support for the EFMA, once the transition begins.

Chapter IV of the ARCSS calls for the establishment of an Advisory Committee, charged with advising and building the capacity of the EFMA, as well as assessing and reviewing the effectiveness of the EFMA's oversight functions. The ARCSS outlines that membership of the Advisory Committee will include representatives from three major donors. Once the EFMA is established, we are well-positioned, as the largest donor, to assume one of the three donor representative positions and to play an active role on the committee.

Question. The U.N. panel of experts report states that "obstruction of humanitarian assistance and of peacekeeping operations has ... escalated since the adoption of resolution 2206." Executive Order 13664 authorizes targeted sanctions against individuals or leaders who obstruct the delivery or distribution of humanitarian assistance.

- Have we identified anyone for sanctions under this provision?
- Are such sanctions under consideration?

Answer. On July 1, 2015, the Security Council Sudan sanctions committee imposed sanctions under UNSCR 2206 on six individuals responsible for obstructing the peace process, committing violations of international humanitarian law and human rights violations and abuses, and attached against United Nations missions. The committee designated three each from the government and opposition sides: Major-General Marial Chanuong Yol Mangok; Lieutenant-General Gabriel Jok Riak; Major-General Santino Deng Wol; Major-General Simon Gatwech Dual; Major-General James Koang Chuol; and Major-General Peter Gadet. All are subject to a global travel ban and asset freeze under the sanctions resolution. The United States has sanctioned these six individuals under E.O. 13664.We believe additional sanctions, either U.S. sanctions under E.O. 13664 or multilateral sanctions through the U.N. Security Council, could serve as an important tool should implementation of the peace agreement falter, and we are continually assessing the appropriateness of such measures. We are cognizant, however, of the difficulty of obtaining multilateral sanctions without regional support—without which support from the African nations on the Security Council is unlikely—and so generally would seek such support from the Inter-Governmental Authority on Development (IGAD) countries and other influential African States.

Question. The Panel of Experts has also begun investigations into the financing channels used by the parties to prosecute the war. And according to their August interim report, the government and opposition are "'deriving significant financial benefit from the war.'"

- ◆ Do we have any idea who in the government and the opposition are profiting from the conflict?
- ◆ How much has the South Sudanese government invested in assisting war affected communities during the course of this conflict?

Answer. To date, concerted, interagency efforts to monitor and assess the finances of South Sudanese officials and others who may have been profiting through corruption or from the conflict did not yield significant results, due to the obscurity of many officials' finances and the relative lack of information from financial institutions in the region.

The potential for South Sudanese officials and others to profit from ongoing conflict—and the incentive, therefore, to prolong the conflict—is deeply concerning to us, and we continue to seek greater transparency of South Sudan's public finances. We regularly liaise with representatives from non-governmental organizations that are also undertaking efforts to shed light on official corruption in South Sudan.

The government has not invested in assisting war-affected communities. As we have noted numerous times in public statements and private engagement with the government, GORSS funding for basic services was low before the conflict and has declined since December 2013. In many parts of the country, services come entirely from the international donor community, including the United States and its implementing partners. This is an intolerable situation. As we have made clear to the GORSS and the opposition, they must commit their own resources to implementation of the peace agreement, including reconstruction and support to war-affected communities, if we and other nations are going to commit further funding.

RESPONSE TO A QUESTION FOR THE RECORD SUBMITTED TO
MR. JOHN PRENDERGAST BY SENATOR CARDIN.

Question. What sort of help should we be asking for from governments in the region—Kenya, Ethiopia, and Uganda, for example—in recovering assets that are suspected to be stolen, or identifying them in keeping with sanctions?

Answer. We greatly appreciate the opportunity to answer this excellent question, which gets at the heart of two critical issues: a) how to ensure global sanctions designations made are enforced by South Sudan's neighbors and political allies and b) how to ensure that illicit or stolen assets are not shielded by private banks or governments in the region.

It is unfortunately not surprising that we have direct knowledge of sanctions violations, such as witnessing designated individuals traveling in the region. Clearly, the existing U.N. and OFAC designations are not being enforced in the region, and this was entirely predictable. In fact, this was the topic of Neighborhood Watch, an in-depth study by the Enough Project published in June 2015, as fighting was intensifying on the ground. The study found that despite failing peace talks and public threats made at the time by Ethiopia, in particular, there was little actual political will to see sanctions designations against either party. Uganda, a key military ally to the government of South Sudan involved directly in the fighting, openly lobbied against sanctions at the U.N. in New York.

In order to ensure effective assistance from the region, we need to address three underlying concerns: i) need for higher profile and broader designations; ii) lack of political will to enforce any designations; and iii) limited technical capacity and underdeveloped legal and regulatory frameworks even where political will does exist.

At this stage, only six relatively low-level commanders have been sanctioned. Few of these individuals are critical players, and none appear to have access to or be conduits for substantial assets. In order to trigger the type of asset identification and recovery the question refers to, the sanctions regime needs to be more comprehensive.

The issue of political will requires continued and sustained diplomatic outreach at the highest levels by U.S. government officials to convey that this is a priority for us, that there is a willingness to create consequences for regional non-enforcement, i.e. withholding of bilateral assistance, and that we are able to provide political and economic incentives to enhance cooperation on sanctions enforcement, such as increased technical assistance to address the capacity gaps.

This outreach should also emphasize to Kenyan authorities, for instance, that if they want the country to be a banking leader in the region and on the continent, they need to step up their enforcement efforts, including more direct oversight of financial institutions. President Kenyatta recently delivered a sweeping address in which he outlined numerous plans and strategies to develop further their institutional infrastructure to combat corruption and money laundering. The United States should work to ensure that these promises are delivered upon.

On technical capacity and reforming legal and regulatory frameworks, there are several areas where the U.S. can potentially provide assistance. Regional financial intelligence units (FIUs) that collect and share information between governments and banks are key to these efforts. Regional governments are looking for membership in the Egmont group of FIUs and may be open to accepting technical assistance from Treasury to bring their FIUs up to standard. For example, Section 314(a) of the Patriot Act and implementing regulations empower FinCEN to engage directly with financial institutions to pursue information that has been requested by state, federal, or foreign law enforcement agencies. This is a model that regional FIUs should be encouraged to implement fully as a means of advancing asset identification.

The threat of U.S. led investigations is also helpful in this regard, specifically if intelligence community collection requirements were issued that could potentially result in information that would enable FinCEN to assess money-laundering activity in the region, which Kenya, Uganda, and Ethiopia have made promises to combat as part of the counter-terrorism agenda. The intelligence agencies in these three countries should also be requested to provide to the United States any asset-related and travel information connected to sanctioned individuals and other politically exposed persons of interest. This can further assist the investigations of Treasury and other enforcement agencies.

If regional governments provided the type of cooperation necessary to expand the sanctions list to include more effective targets, demonstrate political will to enforce such sanctions, and accept any necessary technical assistance that would create a more seamless international enforcement system, then we believe South Sudanese assets would be more easily traced and returned to the people of this war-torn country that so desperately needs them.

––––––––

RESPONSES TO QUESTIONS FOR THE RECORD SUBMITTED TO
MR. ADOTEI AKWEI BY SENATOR CARDIN

Question. The African Union Commission of Inquiry report was completed in late 2014, but was not released until October of this year.

♦ Do you have any idea why the release was delayed?

Answer. The delay of the release of the report was based on the belief that publication of the report would jeopardize the mediation process facilitated by the Intergovernmental Authority on Development (IGAD).

Question. Are you concerned that the delay is an indication of lack of commitment by the African Union to fulfilling its role under the peace agreement to establish the hybrid court?

Answer. The continual delay in releasing the report stoked disillusionment on the AU's commitment to justice and accountability. However in the Communique of 26 September the AU Peace and Security Council strongly supported the implementation of the Agreement on the Resolution of Conflict in south Sudan (ARCISS, hereinafter referred to as August peace agreement) and especially as it relates to peace, security, stability, justice, reconciliation and healing in South Sudan.

Question. What should the international community be doing to ensure the AU carries through with the report's recommendations?

Answer. Maintain pressure on the AU to implement the recommendations of the report of the AU CISS and lend financial and technical support to this end.

The human rights situation, both in terms of the conflict and in terms of the overall atmosphere in the country, has been challenging, and conditions are deteriorating.

Question. What steps can we take to support an improvement in human rights conditions in the country?

Answer. Ensure and maintain concerted pressure towards Government of South Sudan and the SPLM/A-IO to adhere to the human rights and humanitarian provisions of the August peace agreement and in particular to ensure humanitarian access, facilitate the safe return of internally displaced populations and cooperate with the transitional justice mechanisms including the hybrid court for South Sudan

Support the imposition of sanctions for individuals held responsible for violation human rights and international humanitarian law and also support the imposition of an arms embargo on South Sudan to stem the flow of weapons into the country.

Urge the government of south Sudan to deposit instruments of ratification of the African charter on human and people's rights and the AU convention relating to the specific aspects of Refugee problems in Africa and to also ratify other key human rights treaties.

Support civil society in their work as a public watchdog. This can be done through ensuring legal and institutional reform of particularly the security sector and also ensuring capacity building and support to civil society to be able to effectively monitor and report on human rights violations.

Support the establishment and operationalization of the hybrid court for South Sudan through provision of financial and technical assistance. Also urge for immediate investigations to ensure evidence collection and preservation.

Question. Given the role government forces have played in some of the abuses and the insufficient government efforts to prosecute abuses, how, and when, should the United States reengage with the security sector?

Answer. The USA is part of the stakeholders whose representatives comprise the Ceasefire and Transitional Security Arrangements Monitoring Mechanism (CTSAMM) . The CTSAMM has mandate to monitor and report on the conduct of parties with regard to security arrangements put in place during the transitional period. This includes permanent ceasefire, separation and cantonment of forces. It therefore has an important role to play in ensuring all parties comply with agreed security arrangements,

The USA should identify ways it can engage with the strategic Defence and Security Review Board . The board has mandate to provide a roadmap for security sector reform.

Advocate for the reform of the National Security Service: In March 2015, the Justice Minister announced that the National Security Service Bill, passed by Parliament on October 8 2014, had become law. The law grants the NSS extensive and broad powers of arrest, detention and seizure without adequate safeguard mechanisms or safeguards against abuse and therefore emboldens their misconduct. Cases of enforced disappearances, arbitrary arrests and prolonged detention have escalated since the conflict began with allegations of torture and ill-treatment while in custody.

Question. The war broke out little more than two years after independence. After decades of fighting Khartoum, the people of South Sudan have witnessed unspeakable violence at the hands of their own leaders. I fear that the unprecedented level of brutality may have rendered reconciliation more difficult, if not impossible.

♦ In your opinion, has the level of brutality rendered reconciliation impossible?

Answer. The conflict has indeed affected and damaged the social fabric of the country. It has pitted ethnic groups against each other and has also led to subdivisions within some ethnic groups for instance the Bul Nuer (a section of the Nuer ethnic group) has been fighting alongside the government forces in Unity state against other Nuer communities). Similarly the environment is currently very complex, fragile and highly politicized. There will therefore be no quick fix in reconciling South Sudanese and the many competing narratives/truths that have been put forward in the duration of the conflict. However all South Sudanese recognize the need for reconciliation now or later and there are existing national and community level initiatives that continue to run and need immediate and medium term support. It is also very important that the provisions of the Agreement on the Resolution of Conflict in South Sudan on accountability, justice and reconciliation are implemented to facilitate and enable the process of healing and reconciliation.

The August peace agreement provides for the establishment of the Commission for Truth, Reconciliation and Healing (CTRH) with a mandate to inquire into all conflicts since 2005 to the present and lead efforts to facilitate the process of local and national healing and reconciliation. The establishment and operationalisation of this body is critical towards ensuring reconciliation, truth and justice in South Sudan

Question. What lessons can be applied from past reconciliation efforts in the country?

Answer. The formulation of the National Dialogue for Peace and Reconciliation by the government in 2014 and the SPLM/IO's National Committee for National Reconciliation in the same year, indicated a vested interest in controlling the discourse on truth, justice and accountability. It is important to ensure the process of reconciliation is not seen as an elite driven process. It needs to be both at local and national levels. There is need for public participation especially of conflict affected populations.

Currently, there is a National Platform for Peace and Reconciliation made up of various organisations (churches, civil society, governmental) including the Committee for National Healing, Peace and Reconciliation (CNHPR), the South Sudan Peace and Reconciliation Commission (SSPRC) and Specialised Committee on Peace and Reconciliation (SCPR) in the National Assembly, with a number of civil society groups all seeking to build a movement. The roles of all this bodies will be accommodated by the CTRH when established and the CNHPR in particular, will hand over all its records to the CTRH.

Need to find a holistic approach in which issues of justice and reconciliation are pursued simultaneously and in complement to each other. It is widely recognized that an absence of accountability for past crimes/atrocities in South Sudan has contributed to the current conflict. The August Peace agreement provides for the establishment of a hybrid court for South Sudan, the aforementioned CTRH and Compensation and Reparations Authority.

Provision of mental health care services: Decades of conflict since 1983 have had a huge impact on the mental health and wellbeing of South Sudanese populations. A 2007 study carried out in Juba by Bayard Roberts, the director of the Centre for Health and Social Change at the London School of Hygiene and Tropical Medicine, found high levels of mental distress among the population surveyed. Thirty-six per cent of respondents met symptom criteria for Post-Traumatic Stress Disorder (PTSD) and 50% of those surveyed met symptom criteria for depression. The study showed a direct correlation between a traumatic event such as being injured or forcefully evicted with the likelihood of PTSD and depression.

More recently, a survey of 1,525 South Sudanese people in conflict areas carried out by the South Sudan Law Society (SSLS) and the U.N. Development Programme (UNDP) between October 2014 and April 2015 found that 41% of respondents exhibited symptoms consistent with a diagnosis of PTSD. Another survey conducted by the SSLS in the Bor PoC site showed that almost all respondents reported suffering ongoing trauma, stress and poor mental health since an attack on the UNMISS PoC site in April 2014.

Despite the staggering numbers, survivors of atrocities committed by both sides to the conflict are not receiving adequate mental health care support either within the protection of civilian sites or outside. Mental health is a particularly neglected component of the health sector in South Sudan yet addressing the mental health issues associated with the conflict and ensuring trauma healing is not only essential for the process of reconciliation but can lend to long term country stability.

————

RESPONES TO QUESTIONS FOR THE RECORD SUBMITTED TO
MR. BOB LEAVITT BY SENATOR CARDIN

Question. The Agreement on the Resolution of the Conflict in the Republic of South Sudan calls for the establishment of a national Commission of Truth, Reconciliation and Healing.

♦ When do we expect the Commission to come on line?
♦ What programs does the United States government have at the grassroots to promote reconciliation?
♦ What role can the U.S. government play in ensuring that our programs further the work of the Commission once it is up and running?
♦ What lessons can be applied from past reconciliation efforts to ensure sustainable healing of communities?

Answer. According to the Agreement, legislation mandating the creation of the national Commission of Truth, Reconciliation and Healing (CTRH) must be passed within six months of the establishment of the Transitional Government of National Unity and must commence activities no later than a month after passage of that legislation. As the Agreement's implementation is behind schedule, the Transitional Government has not yet been established. The Joint Monitoring and Evaluation Commission, which was created to oversee implementation of the agreement, released a timetable in November calling for the formation of the Transitional Government of National Unity by January 22.

USAID has a long history of supporting grassroots peace and reconciliation efforts in South Sudan, including prior to and during the Comprehensive Peace Agreement interim period (2005-2011) and independence. In the lead up to independence, USAID opened a small program in then-southern Sudan with the goal of mitigating local-level conflict along key national fault lines through grassroots-level peace dialogues with communities, traditional authorities, and local officials as entry points toward reconciliation. When the conflict broke out in December 2013, USAID shifted the program to prioritize grassroots efforts led by civil society, community groups, and others aimed at preventing the spread of conflict and supporting grassroots resilience to political-military pressures. In the current context, the program continues to focus on these areas. In coordination with other donors, USAID is currently exploring additional opportunities to support various reconciliation efforts led by South Sudan's active faith-based community and traditional leaders to advance grassroots reconciliation in 2016.

When the CTRH becomes active and demonstrates its credibility and independence, the U.S. government plans to support the Commission's efforts through direct or technical support. The U.S. government may also continue to work to support other transitional justice mechanisms, including the hybrid court, to redress the atrocities committed during the conflict and promote long-term, sustainable peace.

From past peace-building and reconciliation programming in post-conflict contexts as well as past efforts in South Sudan, we have learned that the work of any truth and reconciliation commission must be based upon:

♦ Transparency, independence, and impartiality: Truth and reconciliation work must be viewed as legitimate in the eyes of the South Sudanese, must be free from political manipulation, must treat all sides equally, and must be open to public scrutiny. If one side is ignored or the process is manipulated, the process of truth-telling and healing will be significantly hampered, and the recommendations of the CTRH will lack legitimacy.

♦ Consultation: All processes should involve consultation with a wide array of stakeholders at all stages, including civil society, victims' groups, women, youth and other marginalized groups. Building a national consensus through citizen involvement, buy-in and ownership will encourage greater participation and sustainability.

♦ Trauma healing: Reconciliation work should be paired with efforts that address the needs of victims to heal, interrupt the cycles of violence and build resilience.

Question. Chapter III of the Agreement calls for the establishment of a Special Fund for Reconstruction within a month of the transition which is supposed to assess and determine the priorities for reconstruction. It calls for a representative from the Troika, of which the U.S. is a member, to participate.

♦ Has the fund been set up?
♦ Is the administration planning on making a financial contribution to the fund?
♦ Do we plan to send a representative to sit on the Board of Special Reconstruction set up in the agreement?

Answer. The Special Reconstruction Fund (SRF) has not yet been established, nor has the Transitional Government of National Unity, a precondition for establishment of the SRF. As provided by the peace agreement, the United States shall have one seat on the SRF Board, as will Norway and the United Kingdom, our Troika partners. The Administration is prepared to support reconstruction efforts provided that South Sudanese leaders show a commitment of their own to implementing the agreement and, in the case of the SRF, a commitment of funds to rebuilding their country. We have not yet determined whether we will provide a financial contribution to the SRF.

Question. Forty humanitarian workers have been killed since the onset of the fighting. Compounds of relief agencies have been broken into, humanitarian workers harassed, and there have been reports of sexual assaults against aid workers. Despite the dire humanitarian situation, the government still appears to want to move forward with a bill to govern the operation of NGOs that has some humanitarian organizations worried.

♦ Has the government investigated and prosecuted anyone for assaults on humanitarian workers or for breaking in and looting compounds of humanitarian organizations?
♦ What efforts has Ambassador Phee made to press the government to investigate these incidents?

Answer. We are not aware of any investigations or prosecutions undertaken by the government of South Sudan in response to these crimes.

Ambassador Phee regularly raises the importance of the role played by the U.N. Mission in the Republic of South Sudan (UNMISS) and other U.N. agencies, as well as the contributions of humanitarian organizations, with senior officials at the national and state level. She has called on government officials to create a secure operating environment for humanitarian actors and to investigate and prosecute those responsible for committing crimes against humanitarian personnel and assets. She has discussed this issue on multiple occasions with Inspector General of Police General Pieng Deng Kuol Arap, Sudan People's Liberation Army Chief of General Staff Paul Malong and state governors. She regularly meets with humanitarian actors to ascertain their concerns and priorities to ensure she remains an informed advocate on their behalf and has used her engagements with the media to advance support for the U.N. and humanitarian organizations.

In addition, Deputy Assistant Secretary for State/PRM Catherine Wiesner and I visited South Sudan in October to review the humanitarian situation in the country. We met with representatives of various U.N. agencies, diplomatic heads of mission, non-governmental organizations, and government officials. This high-level visit drew attention to the challenges facing the humanitarian response, as well as aid personnel operating in the country. South Sudanese officials reiterated their commitment to implementing the peace agreement and pledged to work to address issues of access and safety for humanitarian workers in the country. Ambassador Phee has continued to follow up on this commitment and urged government officials to take necessary measures to ensure the safety and security of all humanitarian aid workers in South Sudan.

Question. In 2015, UNMISS, the AU and Human Rights Watch released reports alleging government and opposition forces and their allies gang raped and abducted young girls and women during fighting. Under the terms of the peace deal, the perpetrators of this violence and their superiors must be held to account for these crimes by the Hybrid Court. In the meantime, thousands of women are isolated in insecure areas in dire need of medical and psychological help.

♦ How is the U.S. working with other donors to improve the provision of health, psychosocial, legal and economic services for survivors of violence?

♦ What percentage of women and girls can be reached with such services? Do we have a plan to increase the number of people we are reaching? Do we have adequate resources to meet the need?

Answer. The U.S. Government coordinates closely with other humanitarian and development donors and stakeholders, both at the headquarters level and in Juba, to ensure that resources are used as effectively as possible to address needs in South Sudan. This donor engagement includes coordinating to ensure that all implementers take the needs of women, girls and other vulnerable groups into account and that programs are designed in a way that is safe and accessible to those in need of assistance and does not exacerbate existing risks. USAID remains committed to ensuring that survivors of violence are able to access the care they need. Our programs include creating safe spaces for traumatized women, clinical management of rape, psychosocial counseling and reunification of children separated from their families during the violence.

USAID programs work to prevent and address the effects of gender-based violence (GBV) through its water, sanitation and hygiene (WASH) and Emergency Education programs. USAID and UNICEF have partnered on a three-year program to improve safe access to water, sanitation and hygiene facilities among internally displaced populations and other vulnerable communities. The program has incorporated activities to prevent and respond to GBV and reaches more than 189,000 people in seven states. Since May 2014, USAID and UNICEF have partnered to provide emergency education to children forced to flee their homes due to conflict in South Sudan. The partnership will benefit 200,000 children, including 80,000 girls. The aim of the project is to provide safe learning spaces and gender-segregated sanitation facilities, mitigate the psychological effects of conflict and violence on children, train teachers in psychosocial support, support out-of-school youth and adolescents with an accelerated learning program including life skills, and disseminate information on self-protection, including protection against GBV, health, and peace education.

Due to sensitivities around reporting sexual and gender-based violence that are exacerbated during times of conflict, it is impossible to know the exact number of people who have experienced these crimes and require aid. However, we do know that thousands of displaced people, particularly in Unity and Upper Nile states, remain inaccessible or infrequently accessible due to insecurity. USAID is actively working to increase the reach of our partners by exploring ways to safely expand mobile and community-based services for women and girls, although scaling up these services will only be possible if the security situation allows. We have also been working with our diplomatic colleagues to advocate with state and local officials for unhindered access to populations in need. Following these conversations, UNMISS has established a temporary operating base in Leer County, Unity State, in an effort to provide a protective presence in one of the areas that has been hardest to reach throughout the conflict. In addition, a recent aid mission to the most conflict-affected counties in Unity State has enabled humanitarian organizations to more thoroughly assess acute needs, begin emergency response interventions and plan for sustained and increased service provision where access and security conditions allow.

The 2015 South Sudan Humanitarian Response Plan, which outlines the humanitarian community's funding requests for the year, requested $60 million for protection activities. As of mid-December, international donors had provided approximately $39 million for protection activities, amounting to 65 percent of the request.

Question. The State Department has documented violations of democratic freedoms since 2012, including "corruption, harassment of nongovernmental organizations (NGOs) and attacks on their workers, illegal detentions, intimidation of journalists, and detention by security forces."

  ♦ As I understand it, there is nearly $25 million available this fiscal year for democracy and governance programming in South Sudan. How are we going to use that money? Have we been able to effectively program such funds in the midst of the conflict?

Answer. The $25 million in Economic Support Funds (ESF) for democracy and governance programming in South Sudan is shared between USAID and State Department with a goal of promoting peace, reducing conflict, building and protecting independent media, supporting reconciliation, enabling local resilience and furthering access to justice.

While the conflict has presented challenges to democracy and governance and peacebuilding programs, USAID has continued to effectively program such funds in an increasingly polarized environment. Despite these challenges, USAID assistance over the last two years of civil war has enabled nascent civil society actors to promote dialogue on key issues related to implementation of the peace agreement and governance issues, such as sensitization on the content of the peace agreement, advocacy on contentious legislation, such as the NGO Bill, and build internal organizational capacity. In addition, USAID support to community and FM radio has extended the reach of free and independent information to communities affected and divided by conflict. Also, due to USAID's long-standing ties to South Sudanese communities that pre-date the current conflict, our nimble operating partners have been able to build trust with communities and effectively program sensitive activities that pursue peace and strengthen the voice of the South Sudanese. USAID remains closely engaged with local stakeholders and international partners to exploit windows of opportunity that exist and emerge as the implementation of the August 2015 peace agreement progresses.

USAID's democracy and governance funding, roughly $23.5 million of the $25 million, will be used to support ongoing and emergent initiatives aimed at reducing inter- and intra-communal tension, building trust and preventing the further spread of local-level conflict, as well as continued support to civil society and the media to counter closing political space. Through established programs, USAID will use democracy and governance funds to promote access to reliable information for communities, including in critical geographic areas, in order to counter political manipulation and misinformation that could lead to further tensions and conflict. USAID will continue its support to Eye Radio, a network of community radio stations that broadcast mostly in local languages and the Humanitarian Information Service, which provide information to populations displaced by conflict. Simultaneously, USAID will expand radio coverage and transition these media outlets to local, South Sudanese ownership to ensure sustainability. Eye Radio was the only South Sudanese media outlet to provide live coverage of the peace negotiations in Addis Ababa, and the USAID-funded radio network is critical to disseminating balanced and accurate information on a range of peace and development issues in South Sudan.

USAID support to civil society will advance its capacity to participate in political processes, including implementation of the peace agreement, and provide civic education to counter ethnic polarization. USAID will continue to train civil society organizations to operate in an insecure environment and to provide safe meeting space and Internet access through an expanding network of Civic Engagement Centers around the country (currently operating in Juba and Wau, and planned to open soon in Yambio). Additionally, these funds will be used to help communities mitigate disputes, promote peace messages and strengthen tools and resources necessary to build trust and resolve problems without resorting to violence. Funds will also advance important peacebuilding and reconciliation efforts. Illustrative activities include civil society monitoring of and disseminating objective information about the peace agreement, providing logistical support to locally driven peace initiatives and expanding trade as means to strengthen positive inter-communal relationships.

USAID will also use these programs to lay the foundation for healing and reconciliation by helping communities understand how trauma has perpetuated historical tensions and identify internal divisions that hinder their ability to reconcile. USAID is currently exploring additional opportunities to support reconciliation efforts through engagement of faith-based leaders and organizations.

The Department of State, though the Office of the U.S. Special Envoy manages a portion of the Democracy and Governance ESF funding, which will be utilized to support human rights abuse investigation and documentation or the establishment of a credible accountability mechanism, such as a hybrid court per the Agreement on the Resolution of Conflict in South Sudan. In addition, INCLE funds are used to support Rule of Law and Justice programming, including a grant that trains paralegals to provide legal guidance to South Sudanese citizens in rural areas and communities who seek justice through local and traditional mechanisms. Pending final negotiations of the transitional security arrangements, State Department's Bureau for International Narcotics and Law Enforcement is also considering projects to assist rule of law mechanisms to support security and justice during the transition, including detention facilities and legal processes for individuals arrested or detained by the new Joint Integrated Police.

RESPONSES TO QUESTIONS FOR THE RECORD SUBMITTED TO
AMBASSADOR PRINCETON LYMAN BY SENATOR CARDIN

Question. To date, few of the provisions of the peace agreement have been implemented. It is unclear that the leaders of either of the warring factions are committed to full implementation.

♦ Can the country ever move forward politically with Salva Kiir and Riek Machar part of the leadership, or must they step aside in order for a sustainable peace in the country?

♦ What steps can the United States and International Community take to

Answer. It is questionable that either Salva Kiir or Riek Machar could regain the credibility and support to lead the country through the kind of transformation that the country needs. This is especially true given the ethnic violence with which both have been associated. Nevertheless, to end the fighting it was deemed necessary by IGAD to bring the two together in a transitional government. Both will try to use that opportunity to position themselves for a presidential run in the next election. The way to ease them out of that expectation would, in my view, to bring forward the work of the Hybrid Court to begin investigation and adjudication of the crimes cited in the Commission of Inquiry report. In that process, while other transformation steps take place, it should become clear that each of these leaders has forfeited the right to run and must step aside, indeed that their running could reignite the conflict. JMEC should use its authority to persuade or disqualify them.

But others around them should also be dealt with by the Court, making room for a fresh set of candidates in the next election.

Question. Given the role government forces have played in some of the abuses and the insufficient government efforts to prosecute abuses, how, and when, should the United States reengage with the security sector? What conditions should the United States put in place before starting security sector reform?

Answer. Security sector reform will be extremely difficult to implement until there is a clear path toward political reformation and a process of reconciliation. In the meanwhile, troops will need to be cantoned. There, they can be counted, organized for DDR, and given the options of registering to return to civilian life. Once it is possible to begin the DDR process, it would be better for the U.N. to take the lead. It would be difficult for the US to clear almost any of the current forces under the Leahy guidelines making US engagement quite difficult.

Question. How can we ensure that DDR is fully implemented in the wake of the peace agreement? What specific lessons can be applied from past DDR processes in South Sudan?

Answer. DDR failed earlier in South Sudan because (a) the government was still engaged in border disputes and confrontation with Sudan, and (b) the SPLA was in fact a confluence of militia, each under the command of an autonomous general, which was the way Kiir united the country before the referendum. Thus neither the government, nor the individual militia commanders were prepared to cut back their own forces. I doubt there will be much of any progress on DDR until a new political dispensation has been established, assurances made to various ethnic groups that their grievances will be addressed, and the U.N. given the authority and the resources to carry it out. Even then, it will take years, and the overall JMEC structure should remain in place to monitor it throughout that time.

Question. The problem of grand corruption is not unique to South Sudan, but it is certainly one of the underlying factors contributing to the current conflict.

♦ What specific actions should the Transitional Government take to establish financial transparency mechanisms?
♦ What steps should the United States government take to support these efforts?

Answer. The peace agreement provides for an oversight mechanism for financial management, on which the US and other donors have a seat. But the Transitional Government, under Kiir and Machar, still has considerable operating authority over the budget. I would rather have seen an independent management for revenue and budgeting. The US will have to be vigorous and demanding in pressing the planned oversight role and prepared to ask for strengthening it at the first sign of serious corruption. The U.N. sanctions committee should also be asked to continue its investigations into obstacles to the peace, with special attention to any arms purchases being made by wither side. Such purchases in themselves should be occasion for establishing stronger outside management. Ideally, but difficult to get both China and Sudan to agree, oil proceeds—the principle revenue for the government—should be put in escrow and released only under international direction.

○